MW01532071

CRYPTOCURRENCIES

SAVINGS AND INTEREST

ECONOMIC GROWTH

MONEY
for Curious Kids

An illustrated introduction to spending and
saving, finance, economics—and more!

SUPPLY AND DEMAND

CORRUPTION

ARCTURUS

ARCTURUS

This edition published in 2025 by Arcturus Publishing Limited
26/27 Bickels Yard, 151–153 Bermondsey Street,
London SE1 3HA

Copyright © Arcturus Holdings Limited

All rights reserved. No part of this publication may be reproduced, stored in a retrieval
system, or transmitted, in any form or by any means, electronic, mechanical, photocopying,
recording, or otherwise, without prior written permission in accordance with the
provisions of the Copyright Act 1956 (as amended). Any person or persons who do any
unauthorized act in relation to this publication may be liable to criminal prosecution and
civil claims for damages.

Author: Claudia Martin
Illustrator: Nik Neves
Consultant: Tejvan Pettinger
Designer: Dani Leigh
Editor: Lydia Halliday
Managing Designer: Rosie Bellwood-Moyler
Managing Editor: Joe Harris

ISBN: 978-1-3988-3339-5
CH011575NT
Supplier 29, Date 0225, Print run 00008293

Printed in China

CONTENTS

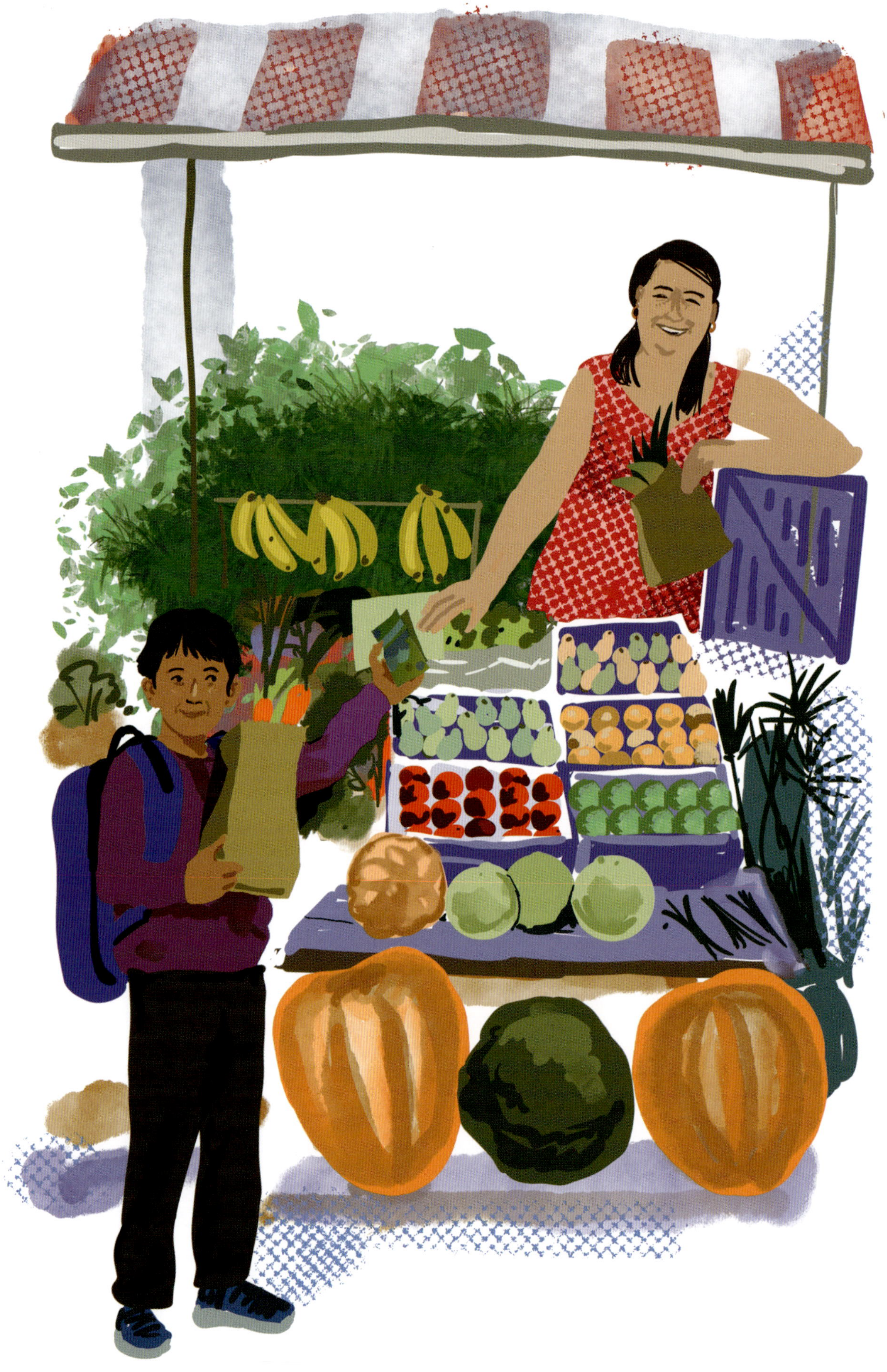

WELCOME TO THE WORLD OF MONEY

Money is the coins and banknotes you hand over when you're buying books in a store. Money is the numbers on a computer screen that tell a worker they've been paid. Money is what everyone worries about when they don't have enough to pay a bill. Money is what adults save slowly, week by week, so they can take the trip of a lifetime. Money matters to everyone, whether they like it or not!

You will become a money expert as you journey through the pages of this book. You'll learn how **economists** try to keep countries wealthy and healthy. You'll find out how **bank** managers keep their customers' money safe. You'll discover how businesspeople make their companies grow. And you'll delve into how **stock** brokers know when to sell, sell, sell!

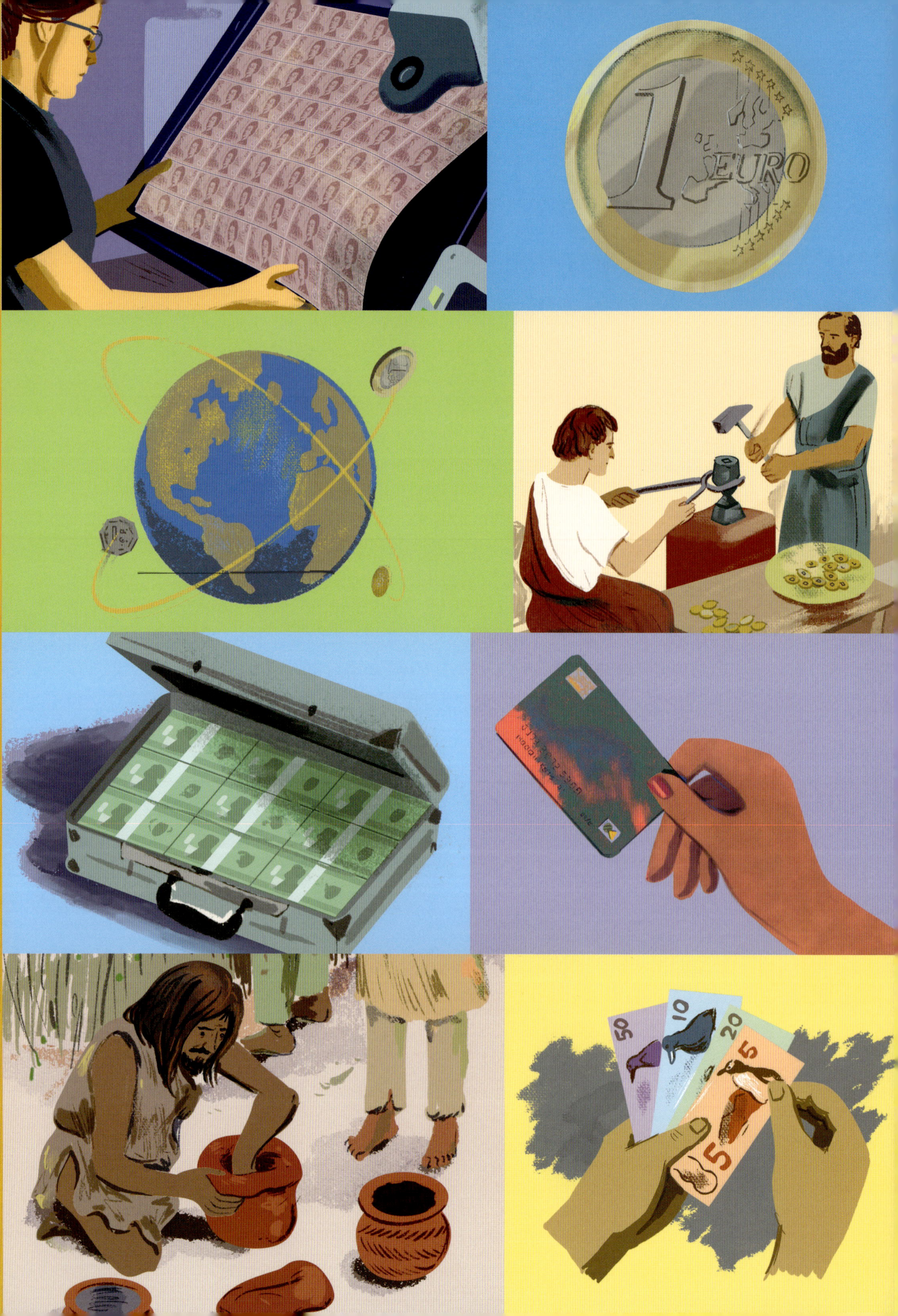
1
EURO
50
10
20
5

CHAPTER 1

WHAT IS MONEY?

Money is all about trust. Coins, notes, and plastic payment cards have no real value. They cost very little to make, so—in themselves—they are nearly worthless. However, everybody agrees that coins, notes, and plastic cards can be used to pay for things. This means that, when someone gives you a coin, you trust that you can use it as payment. Everybody else has the same trust. This trust is all that gives money its value.

In this chapter, we'll find out when and why that trust began to form. We'll learn how money has developed over the centuries, making us switch from trusting in coins made of gold to trusting in numbers on a computer screen. We'll discover how that trust can be shaken by money crimes.

STARTING WITH BARTERING

Money has not always existed. When people hunted for their own food and made their own clothes and shelters, there was no need for money. Then some people began to **barter**, which is when food or **goods** are swapped for things of equal value. This was the start of something special!

BARTERING

There was not much need for bartering before around 10,000 years ago. This was when some people learned to collect and sow seeds, so they settled down as farmers. Before then, people were "hunter-gatherers" who caught or found their food, usually while following animal herds across the land.

Once people settled in one place, a few people specialized in particular skills, such as making clay pots. Now, some farmers might want to swap food for a pot. Strict bartering was usually done only between strangers. Most of the time, people just trusted that, if they gave their cousin a pot, they would eventually get a gift in return.

?

OUT OF CURIOSITY

Huge stone disks, up to 4 m (12 ft) wide, are sometimes used as money on the Pacific Island of Yap. Since most disks are too heavy to lift, their ownership changes in name only.

COMMODITY MONEY

Gifting and bartering were awkward if a potter wanted to swap their vase for fish, loaves, and wool supplied by three different people. This was why money was invented! The first forms of money were **commodities**. A commodity is a material or natural resource, such as barley, animal skins, or shells. Just like today's money, these commodities had an agreed value and were used as a **medium of exchange**—an item that can be exchanged for goods.

Unlike most modern money, however, commodity money usually had a value in itself—because barley can be eaten, skins can be worn, and shells are pretty ornaments—as well as a value in buying other goods.

Cattle were probably the first commodity to be used as payment, perhaps as early as 9000 BCE, not long after the first wild cattle were captured by humans.

From around 3000 BCE, barley was used as money by **traders** in Mesopotamia, which was in the region of modern-day Iraq.

Cowries, which are the shells of sea snails, were used in China from around 1200 BCE. Later, cowries were spent by traders across Africa, Australia, and eastern and southern Asia, up until the 20th century in parts of Africa and on some islands.

From around 1025 BCE, small metal models of the tools that had previously been used for barter—such as spades, hoes, and knives—were used as money in China.

COINS

A coin is a small object, usually round, flat, and metal, that is used as money. Early coins were a form of commodity money, since their precious metals had a value in themselves. Today's coins are made of inexpensive metal so they are a form of **fiat money**.

EARLIEST COINS

The value of commodity money could not always be trusted: A shell was not valued everywhere, while barley lost value as it rotted. Using metal bars or chunks became a solution, because metal was a commodity that was widely valued and did not decay. Metal coins were an even better invention, since they were small and easy to carry.

In around 590 BCE, some of the earliest coins were made in Lydia, in modern-day Turkey. Like most later coins, Lydian coins were made by the country's government, bore a symbol of that government (a lion), and were put into **circulation** by the government.

LYDIAN LION COIN

MINTS

Most coins, both ancient and modern, are made in a **mint**. Mints are run by governments, which means that coins can be trusted. Mints ensure that coins have standard sizes, weights, and designs, which are proof that the coin was made in an official mint. They also make the right amount of coins to replace damaged ones and to meet people's needs.

IN AN ANCIENT ROMAN MINT, METAL WAS MELTED, POURED INTO A MOLD TO FORM FLAT DISKS, THEN TRIMMED.

DESIGNS

Coins are said to have an observe side, which often features the head of a monarch, important person, or national symbol; and a reverse side, with a range of different designs. The year of minting and **face value** may be shown on either side. Most coins are round, but a few are polygons, with several equal sides. Different designs and metals are used for different face values.

ROMAN 25 DENARII, 27–18 BCE, WITH HEAD
OF REIGNING EMPEROR AUGUSTUS

BRITISH 1 PENNY, 1861, WITH HEAD
OF REIGNING QUEEN VICTORIA

UNITED STATES 50 CENTS, 2015, WITH HEAD
OF PRESIDENT JOHN F. KENNEDY (1917–63)

FIAT MONEY

Early coins were made of valuable metals such as gold or silver. During the 20th century, nearly all the world's mints switched to using low-value, common metals such as nickel, copper, zinc, and iron. This makes modern coins a form of fiat money, which has value only because people agree it can be used as a medium of exchange.

A STAMP WAS POUNDED INTO EACH DISK USING A HAMMER, LEAVING AN IMPRESSION OF THE DESIGN.

OUT OF CURIOSITY

The current United States 1 dollar coin has a melt value—the cost of the metal it contains—of around 6 cents, which is 6 percent of its face value.

BANKNOTES

Also known as bills, paper money, or notes, today's banknotes are a form of fiat money. Banknotes are used for higher-value money units—such as dollars, euros, and pounds—while coins are used for low-value units, such as cents and pence.

I PROMISE TO PAY

The first paper money was issued in 7th-century China. These notes—and most banknotes for the next several centuries—were merchants' promissory notes, which stated that they promised to pay the holder an amount of precious metal if the note was presented to a certain bank or other named authority. These notes took away the need for merchants to carry heavy loads of coins.

NATIONAL NOTES

By 1024, the Chinese government had become the first government to issue notes, which promised to pay the holder in coins at a later date. Until the mid-20th century, national banknotes could still be taken to a bank and swapped for precious metal equal to their face value. Today, that is no longer the case. Today's banknotes have value only because we believe they do.

NEW ZEALAND NOTES

LEGAL TENDER

Along with coins, banknotes are legal tender. Legal tender is any form of payment that a court of law recognizes as acceptable payment for a **debt**. In most countries, law courts recognize the country or region's coins and banknotes as legal tender, but foreign banknotes and coins, payment cards, and other forms of non-**cash** payment are not recognized.

OUT OF CURIOSITY

In 1988, Australia was the first country to issue notes made from plastic polymer. On average, paper notes survived for two years, but polymer notes last at least twice as long.

NATIONAL CURRENCIES

Japanese yen, Nigerian naira, and Australian dollars are **currencies**. A currency is the system of money—including particular coins and notes—that is used in a country. A currency is usually decided by a country's government and accepted as payment only within certain boundaries.

CURRENCY COUNT

Most countries and some **territories** have their own currency. However, there are only 180 currencies, but more than 195 countries and territories. Some countries share a currency as part of a currency union, which helps people to trade and travel smoothly. The largest currency union is the euro, which is the currency of 20 European countries.

However, some entirely separate currencies share a similar name. For example, dollar is the name of more than 25 different currencies, including the Australian, Canadian, New Zealand, and United States dollars.

1 EURO COIN, 2007

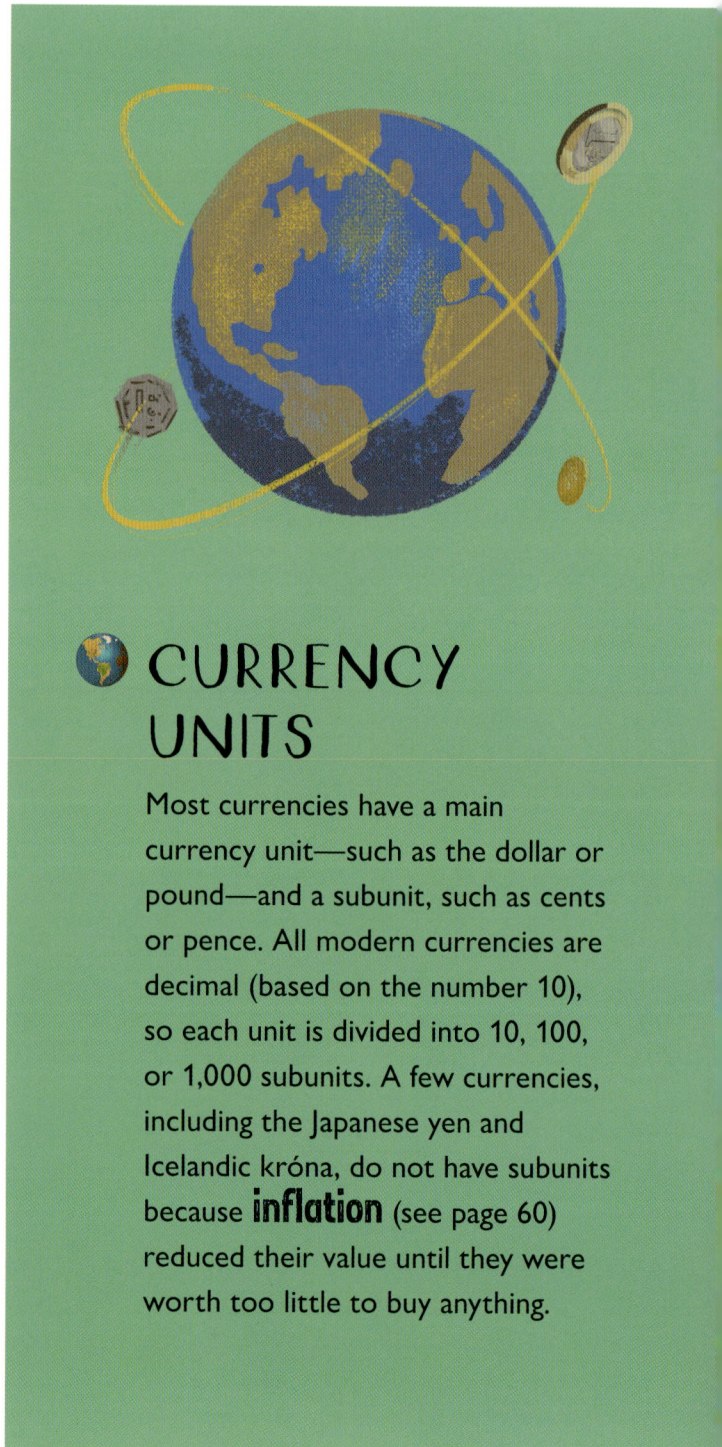

CURRENCY UNITS

Most currencies have a main currency unit—such as the dollar or pound—and a subunit, such as cents or pence. All modern currencies are decimal (based on the number 10), so each unit is divided into 10, 100, or 1,000 subunits. A few currencies, including the Japanese yen and Icelandic króna, do not have subunits because **inflation** (see page 60) reduced their value until they were worth too little to buy anything.

OUT OF CURIOSITY

The United States dollar is also an official currency of more than seven other countries, including East Timor, Ecuador, El Salvador, Marshall Islands, Micronesia, Palau, and Panama.

PEOPLE NEED TO CHANGE CURRENCY WHEN THEY TRAVEL FROM ONE CURRENCY ZONE TO ANOTHER.

🌎 EXCHANGE RATES

An **exchange rate** is the value at which one currency can be swapped for another. For example, 1 Canadian dollar may be swapped for 110 Japanese yen. A few governments choose to fix their currency to one or more valuable currencies, such as the United States dollar, so its exchange rate with that currency does not change. This helps the currency of a smaller or more unstable country to stay valuable.

Most currencies are floating, which means that they can be bought and sold freely on the foreign exchange market, which is a computerized system that allows traders such as banks to buy and sell currencies. The exchange rates of floating currencies change daily, with the cost of a currency going up as the country has **financial** successes and down when it has setbacks.

ELECTRONIC MONEY

Today, many people make and receive all their payments without touching coins and banknotes. They are using **electronic money**, which is a record of money that is usually held on bank computer systems.

CHANGE THE RECORD

Many people are paid for their work in electronic money rather than in banknotes. When this happens, a record is made on their bank's computer system that a payment of electronic money has gone into that person's **bank account**. The money can then be spent electronically, for example by using a plastic payment card or by typing in bank account details on a website.

Even though electronic money may only ever exist as numbers in computer records, electronic money recorded in a bank account can be turned into coins and notes by making a **withdrawal** over the bank's counter or from an **automated teller machine (ATM)**, also called a cash machine.

PLASTIC CARDS

Different types of plastic payment cards, including **debit** and **credit** cards (see page 36), are issued by banks. Most payment cards contain a **microchip** that stores information identifying the card. This can be read by a store's **payment terminal** machine—by tapping, swiping, inserting, or holding the card nearby—or by an ATM. A payment terminal sends a request to the customer's bank, which transfers electronic money into the store's bank account.

PAYING BY APP

Payment **apps** allow electronic payments to be made using a phone. The apps often store the user's payment card details on the phone, then send the information to a payment terminal using **radio waves**. To prevent a stolen phone from being used to make payments, the user proves who they are by typing in a code or by showing the phone their face or fingerprint.

OUT OF CURIOSITY

More than 90 percent of the world's money is electronic, with only around 10 percent of it in the form of banknotes and coins.

DIGITAL CURRENCIES

A **digital currency** is a form of money that is stored and exchanged only on computer systems, such as the internet. Unlike an ordinary currency, which may also be stored on computer systems, a digital currency never takes the form of coins and notes.

CRYPTOCURRENCIES

Cryptocurrencies are digital currencies that can be used to buy things around the world through the internet, without needing to use a bank's services or change one currency for another. Bitcoin and Ether are well-known cryptocurrencies. Even though cryptocurrencies never take physical form, they can buy physical goods and **services**.

BLOCKCHAINS

Each cryptocurrency keeps a record of every **transaction**—the passing of digital "coins" from one person to another—in an electronic record called a blockchain. To stop anyone from changing a blockchain to steal "coins," the blockchain is stored on different computer systems, which must remain identical to be trusted. After a new section of blockchain—called a block—has been filled with around 2,000 transactions, it is closed and encrypted, which means that it is changed into a code that only authorized computers can unlock.

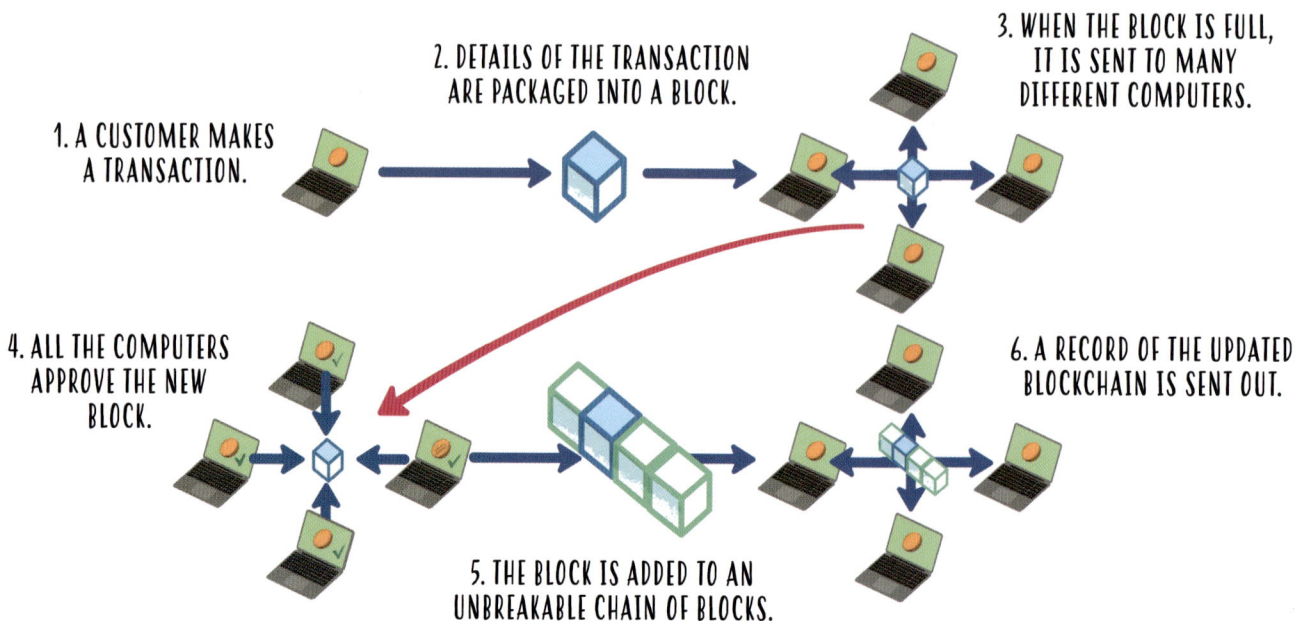

1. A CUSTOMER MAKES A TRANSACTION.

2. DETAILS OF THE TRANSACTION ARE PACKAGED INTO A BLOCK.

3. WHEN THE BLOCK IS FULL, IT IS SENT TO MANY DIFFERENT COMPUTERS.

4. ALL THE COMPUTERS APPROVE THE NEW BLOCK.

5. THE BLOCK IS ADDED TO AN UNBREAKABLE CHAIN OF BLOCKS.

6. A RECORD OF THE UPDATED BLOCKCHAIN IS SENT OUT.

A QUESTION OF TRUST

Cryptocurrencies are issued by businesspeople rather than governments, so some people do not trust them and will not take payment in them. Like most currencies, cryptocurrencies change their value as they are bought and sold by **investors** and traders: When more people buy them, their price rises. However, the value of some cryptocurrencies has fallen dramatically when many people lost trust and sold at once. This makes cryptocurrencies a riskier way to store wealth.

? OUT OF CURIOSITY

There are more than 9,000 cryptocurrencies. Around half of all money invested in cryptocurrencies is in just one of them—Bitcoin.

IN-GAME CURRENCIES

Some digital currencies are accepted only within a particular online game. In-game currencies are used to buy tools, outfits, and boosters in the virtual world. Although these currencies cannot **purchase** items in the "real world," they do have a "real world" cost since they must be bought with ordinary electronic money.

MONEY CRIMES

Criminals commit many different types of financial crimes, both by taking other people's money illegally and by hiding money that has been illegally gained! As with other crimes, people found guilty of serious money crimes are given prison sentences.

COUNTERFEITING

As soon as coins and notes were first made, some people **counterfeited** them, by producing copies to make themselves rich. When coins were still made of precious metals, counterfeiters clipped their edges, collected the metal, and made it into more coins.

Today, counterfeiters focus on banknotes. To prevent counterfeiting, government-approved banknote printers make sure that notes have features that are difficult to copy. These include detailed designs; metallic threads running through the note; and **holographic** panels that show three-dimensional images when they catch the light.

OUT OF CURIOSITY

The most counterfeited currency is the United States dollar, with around 1 in every 10,000 notes in circulation a fake.

🔗 MONEY LAUNDERING

When a criminal makes money by committing a crime, such as selling illegal drugs for cash, they cannot pay their **profit** into a bank, since bankers watch out for people with large amounts of cash. This is where money launderers help out!

Money laundering makes money look as if it came from a legal rather than illegal source. One method is to buy a genuine business, such as a restaurant or store, then pretend the cash was paid to the business by lots of real customers.

🔗 FRAUD

Fraud is a crime that involves deceiving people or organizations to gain money or another benefit. Types of fraud include tricking people into giving their bank account or card information (see page 44); embezzlement, which is when an employee takes money from the business where they work, usually over a period of time; and **tax** evasion, when someone tries not to pay the tax they owe (see page 50).

WEALTH AND POVERTY

What seems wealthy to one person may not seem so to another, because we see "wealth" and "poverty" according to our expectations. However, we can all agree that some people have enough money to live safely and comfortably, while others don't.

WEALTH

Wealth is having plenty of **assets**, which are anything of value, including money, **financial assets**, and possessions. Money may be electronic or banknotes and coins. Financial assets include stocks and **shares** (see page 122). Possessions include anything that can be sold for money, including buildings, land, and cars.

Economists consider wealth in terms of net worth, which is the current value of all assets, minus all debts. People, countries, and regions can be considered wealthy.

ABSOLUTE POVERTY

Absolute poverty is not having enough **income** (money coming in) to meet basic needs, including food, clean water, clothing, shelter, and **sanitation**. According to the **United Nations**, around 10 percent of the world's population lives in absolute poverty. Due to steps forward in technology and government, the number of people in absolute poverty is falling—before the start of the 20th century, the majority of people lived in absolute poverty.

RELATIVE POVERTY

Relative poverty is when a person has less than half the income of the average person in their country. In a wealthy country, someone in relative poverty may be able to meet their basic needs, but they cannot enjoy the same standard of living as others. Standard of living is measured by having access to good schools, jobs, and healthcare, as well as enjoying leisure time.

INEQUALITY

Inequality is the uneven sharing of wealth. Some countries and regions are wealthier than others (see page 56). Within countries, there is also inequality. The wealthiest countries are not the most equal. In the United States, for example, the richest 10 percent of people hold more than two-thirds of all wealth. Slovenia—a country in central Europe with stable government, good schools, and plenty of jobs—has the lowest inequality.

OUT OF CURIOSITY

Around 1 percent of the world's people have almost 50 percent of the world's wealth.

DOES MONEY MATTER?

Everyone knows that the best things in life are free! But does that mean that money never matters? It certainly matters to people when they don't have enough.

WHEN MONEY MATTERS

People living in absolute or relative poverty (see page 22) know that money matters. In Nigeria, where around one-third of people live in absolute poverty, the life expectancy (the average age that people die) is 53. In Japan, one of the world's wealthiest countries, it is 84.

Relative poverty can also affect people's health and happiness. It can reduce people's opportunities to enjoy education and to find rewarding work.

MONEY WORRIES

Even when people do not live in poverty, they may worry about money. They may worry that they do not have enough money to pay bills or college fees. They may worry about the sudden loss of income caused by losing a job. Many people worry about paying back debts. Someone who grew up in poverty may always worry about money, however much they have.

🌺 MONEY AND HAPPINESS

The most joyful things in life—hugging family, laughing with friends—cannot be bought with money. Yet our freedom to enjoy those things without hunger or worries can usually be helped by money. However, does having more money make people happier?

Some **psychologists** say that people with large incomes are, on average, a little more happy than people with low incomes, because they have fewer worries and more opportunities for relaxing. Yet other psychologists say that the happiest people are those with loving relationships, as long as they have enough money to get by.

OUT OF CURIOSITY

Ancient Roman coins were often stamped with a picture of Felicitas, the goddess of happiness, good luck, and success.

CHAPTER 2

BANKS

The earliest known banking took place around 4,000 years ago in the temples of Babylonia, in the region of modern-day Iraq. People took their gold and other valuables to temples, which kept them safe. The temples charged a **fee** for this service, then used this wealth to make **loans**—of seeds—to farmers. When the harvest came in, farmers repaid their loans, plus extra seeds. Details of these loan agreements were pressed into clay tablets, which were baked in the sun to make a record.

In this chapter, we'll take a look at how today's banks carry out the same activities: keeping wealth safe, giving loans, and making records. We'll also find out how banks play their part in keeping money moving, from bank account to account and hand to hand.

WHAT ARE BANKS?

Banks are businesses that accept money paid in by customers, keep it safe, and repay it after being asked. Banks also lend money to customers. Today, much of a bank's work is done with electronic money rather than with coins and notes.

DEPOSITS

A **deposit** is money paid into a bank. Customers can make deposits into a bank account that bears their own name. Deposits are also often made into a person's bank account by their employer, if their salary is paid electronically.

WITHDRAWALS

A withdrawal is money that a customer takes out of their bank account. Over a bank's counter or from an automated teller machine (ATM), also known as a cash machine, a customer can use their payment card to make withdrawals in banknotes. Withdrawals can also be made by paying for purchases with a payment card or by using a bank's website or app: In these cases, electronic money is moved from their account to the account of a business, organization, or person.

WHY USE A BANK?

Since banks are run according to rules (see page 34), they keep money safe. They allow money to be transferred quickly to anyone in the world with a bank account. Due to inventions such as payment cards, banks also remove the need to carry large amounts of cash. In addition, most banks offer advice about **investments** and debts.

(see page 34)

OUT OF CURIOSITY

There are more than 40,000 retail banks in the world, some with just one branch (a local office that customers can visit) and others with branches in many countries.

A BANK IN NAME

When people use the word "bank," they usually mean a **retail bank**, where ordinary people deposit, store, and withdraw money. However, other financial institutions are also called banks but do very different work. Investment banks offer complex services to large businesses, including arranging the buying of other businesses and organizing mergers, which is when two or more companies are combined. **Central banks** (see page 64) are institutions that help governments manage the country's money.

(see page 64)

HOW BANKS MAKE MONEY

Customers deposit money with banks, then banks lend some of that money to people who need to borrow. Yet banks are businesses, so how do they make money to pay their staff and make a profit? Banks make money in three main ways: by collecting **interest**, making investments, and charging fees.

INTERESTING INTEREST

When you borrow money from a bank, you agree to pay interest. Interest is an additional amount to be paid on top of what was originally borrowed—a **percentage** of that amount. Banks also pay interest on money that customers deposit. For example, if you deposited $100 in a bank account that paid 1 percent interest, after one year the bank would pay $1 (1 percent) in interest. If you borrowed $100 at 1 percent interest, you would need to pay an extra 1 percent of what you still owed, every year until you had paid back the full amount.

YEAR 1	YEAR 2	YEAR 3
DEPOSIT: $1,000	TOTAL IN ACCOUNT: $1,010	$1,020.10
PAYMENT OF 1 PERCENT INTEREST: $10	PAYMENT OF 1 PERCENT INTEREST: $10.10	PAYMENT OF 1 PERCENT INTEREST: $10.20

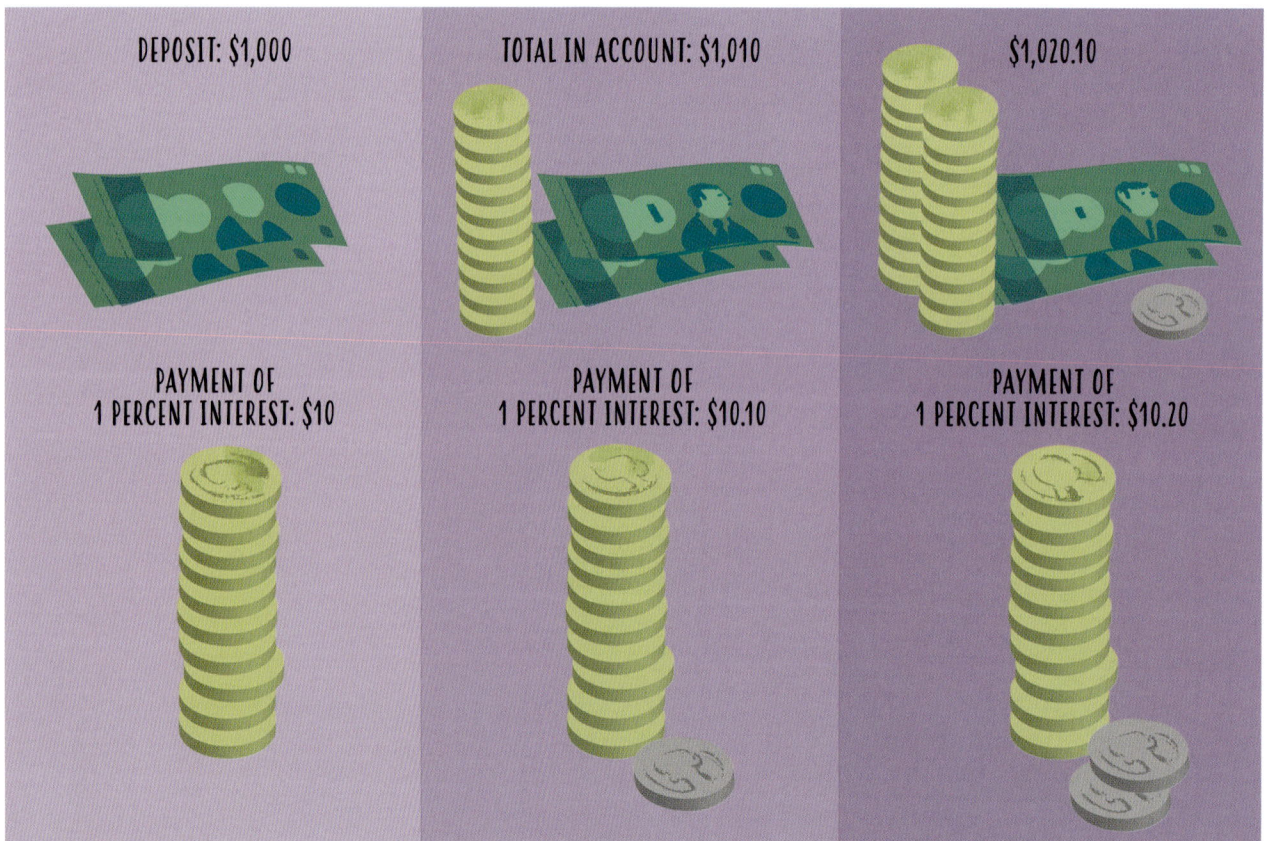

BANKS PAY INTEREST ON THE TOTAL MONEY DEPOSITED IN AN ACCOUNT, INCLUDING THE INTEREST FROM PREVIOUS YEARS. THIS MEANS THAT INTEREST PAID TO CUSTOMERS CAN GROW YEAR AFTER YEAR.

MORE IN, LESS OUT

Banks make money from interest because they always pay their customers a lower rate of interest than they charge to their borrowers. For example, they may pay their customers 1 percent interest, but charge their borrowers 3 percent interest.

BANK RECEIVES 3 PERCENT INTEREST FROM BORROWERS.

BANK PAYS OUT 1 PERCENT INTEREST TO CUSTOMERS.

BANK KEEPS THE DIFFERENCE BETWEEN INTEREST RECEIVED AND PAID OUT.

INVESTING

Banks invest some of the money deposited with them. An investment is something bought in the hope of gaining a profit. Banks try to make very safe investments, often by investing in the government of their own country by buying **bonds**. The government uses the money paid for bonds to help pay for services such as buses and schools. The government pays the bank interest on bonds.

OUT OF CURIOSITY

The oldest bank is the Banca Monte dei Paschi di Siena, which is based in Italy. It has been lending money and accepting deposits since 1472.

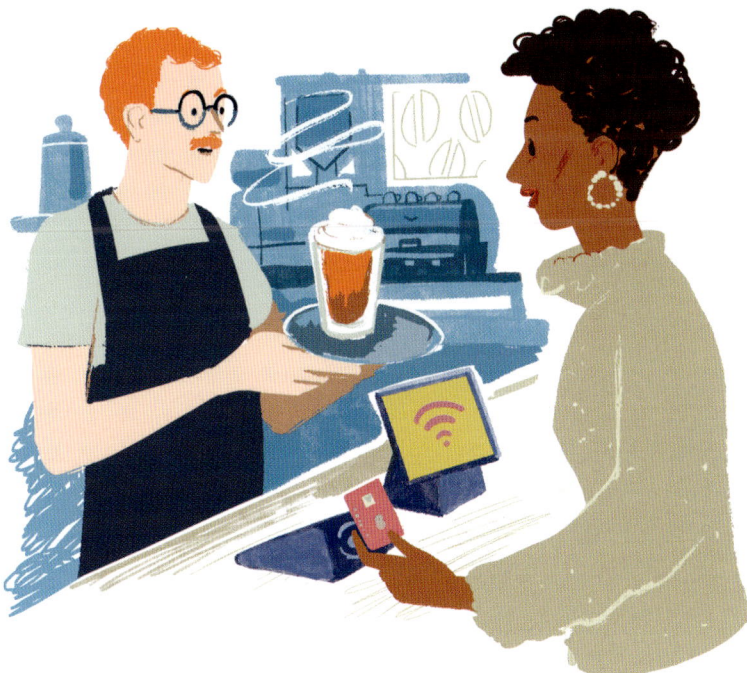

FEES

Banks often charge customers fees for some services, such as opening a bank account or taking out a loan. Many banks also offer debit and credit cards (see page 36). Every time a cardholder uses their card in a store, restaurant, or other business, the store or restaurant pays the bank a small fee.

BANK ACCOUNTS

A bank account is an arrangement between a bank and a customer. The bank keeps an electronic record of the money in a customer's account and allows them to deposit and withdraw money according to the **terms** of the account.

MONEY IN THE BANK

The money in an account is always in the form of electronic money, but it can be turned into banknotes if a customer withdraws it in that form. The amount of money in an account is called the **balance**. A bank account may have a positive balance. Technically, in this case the bank owes money to the customer. However, if the customer owes money to the bank, the account is said to have a negative balance, or an overdraft.

MOST BANKS ALLOW CUSTOMERS TO CHECK THEIR BALANCE ON A WEBSITE.

DATE	DESCRIPTION	WITHDRAWALS	DEPOSITS	BALANCE

ACCOUNT NUMBER

To prevent money from being withdrawn or paid into the wrong account, a bank account is not only identified by the name of the customer but by a long number called an account number. Within each bank, each account number is unique.

TYPES OF ACCOUNTS

Retail banks offer two main types of accounts—**checking** and **savings**. Checking accounts, also known as current or transaction accounts, allow the customer to make withdrawals as often as they want. They come with a debit card (see page 36) for making withdrawals and payments. These accounts pay very little interest.

Savings accounts pay more interest, so they are a good way to store and save money in the long term. They do not offer a debit card. They usually limit the number of withdrawals.

SOME SAVINGS ACCOUNTS ASK CUSTOMERS TO GIVE A WARNING BEFORE MAKING A WITHDRAWAL.

FOR KIDS

Some banks offer accounts for children. Depending on a child's age, these may not offer a debit card or allow the child to make withdrawals without an adult's help. However, they are a great way to save money for the future!

OUT OF CURIOSITY

Around three-quarters of the world's adults have a bank account.

⚠ RULES FOR BANKS ⚠

Helped by their country's central bank, governments make rules that retail banks must obey. These rules help to make sure that customers' money is safe—and can be withdrawn if they need it.

⚠ MONEY IN RESERVE

If banks lent out or invested all the money that customers deposited, they would have a problem. When customers tried to withdraw money, the banks would have little to give them. This is why many banks use a system called fractional-reserve banking. A fraction of deposits—perhaps 10 percent—is held in reserve as "liquid assets," which is either cash or electronic money that can be changed quickly into cash. Many governments set rules for a minimum fraction.

CUSTOMERS DEPOSIT MONEY IN THEIR BANK ACCOUNTS.

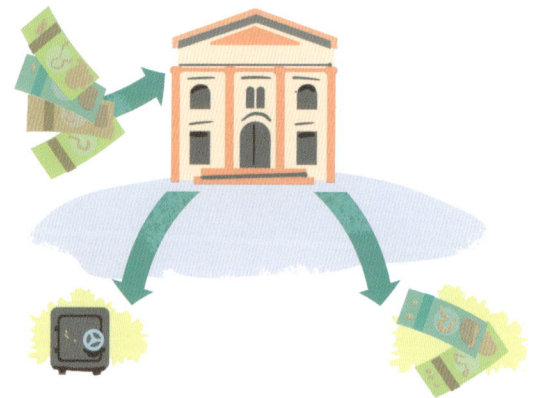

THE BANK KEEPS A FRACTION OF DEPOSITS IN RESERVE.

THE BANK LENDS OR INVESTS THE REST OF ITS DEPOSITS.

⚠ WHAT ARE BANK RUNS?

During a financial crisis or even a natural disaster, there can sometimes be a bank run. This is when lots of people run to the bank and withdraw all their money. This can send more people to the bank, because they worry that the bank's reserves are not big enough for everyone to take their money.

⚠ SAFE FROM BANK RUNS

Today, many governments have protected their customers from bank runs by setting up desposit **insurance** funds, which guarantee that customers will be paid back their money up to a certain, large amount. Every year, banks pay a percentage of their profits into the fund, in case the money is ever needed. This safety net can actually prevent bank runs, because—if people know their money is protected—they don't panic!

⚠ NOT TOO RISKY

All governments say that banks must have enough safe investments, on top of their liquid assets, to balance out risky loans. This rule is known as a **capital** requirement. It helps to make sure that, if lots of people cannot repay the money they have borrowed, the bank does not collapse.

?

OUT OF CURIOSITY

During the 1930s, a worldwide series of bank runs led to customers in the United States alone losing US $7 billion.

DEBIT AND CREDIT CREDITS

There are two main types of plastic payment cards: debit and credit. They both allow people to pay for purchases and to withdraw money in cash. But there is a big difference between the two! When someone uses a debit card, the money leaves their bank account almost instantly. When someone uses a credit card, they pay at a later date.

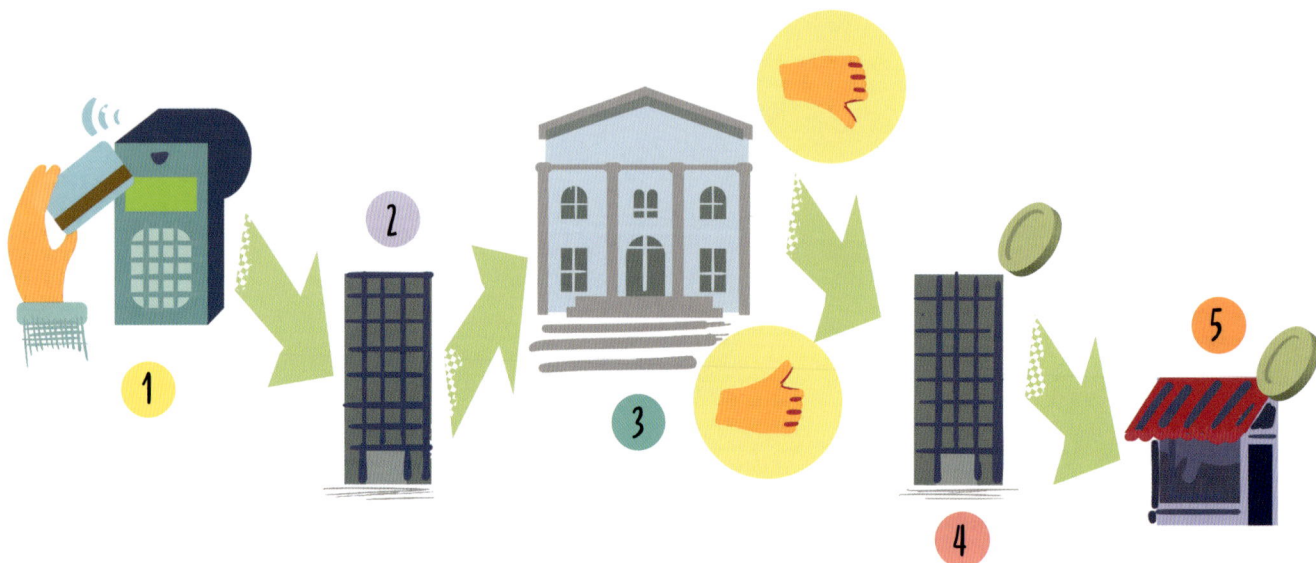

DEBIT CARDS

Debit cards are issued by a bank and linked to a customer's current account, also known as a checking account. Here's what happens when you make a debit card payment in a store:

1. A debit card is tapped, swiped, or inserted in a payment terminal.

2. The payment terminal sends a signal to a card processing company (such as Visa or Mastercard) along wires or through the air as radio waves.

3. The processing company contacts the customer's bank, which checks the customer's account to see if it contains enough money, then accepts or declines (turns down) the payment, usually within a few seconds.

4. Within a day, the customer's bank transfers electronic money from the customer's account to the processing company.

5. The processing company pays the money into the store's bank account, charging the store a small fee for this service.

CREDIT CARDS

Credit cards are also usually issued by banks, but they are linked to a credit account. This is an agreement that allows adults to borrow money from the card issuer up to a certain limit. Credit cards allow adults to buy expensive items, then split the cost over several months.

When a customer pays using a credit card, the process is similar to a debit card, but the money paid to the store comes from the card issuer, not the customer's bank account. Once a month, the card issuer sends the customer a bill for the money they have borrowed. If the customer pays in full, they pay only what they have spent. However, if they leave any money unpaid, they are charged interest.

OUT OF CURIOSITY

Children are not allowed credit cards in their own name, because it would mean signing a legal contract with a card issuer and taking on debt. The law says that kids can't fully take responsibility for either.

HOW CREDIT CARD INTEREST WORKS

Credit card issuers charge interest of up to 30 percent per year. This makes borrowed money harder and harder to pay back. Every day that a bill remains unpaid in full, the card issuer adds interest to the amount owed.

If the yearly interest rate is 30 percent, the daily interest rate is 30 percent divided by 365, which is 0.08 percent. If someone has an unpaid bill on Day 1 of $1,000, they are charged 8 cents for every $100 owed that day, making a total of 80 cents. At the end of Day 1, their new balance is $1,000.80. After a month, with interest added to the growing balance every day, the total money owed would be $1,024.

LOANS

Banks lend money to individuals, couples, and businesses using an agreement called a loan. This arranges the **transfer** of money and how long the customer has to pay it back. Banks don't give loans out of kindness—customers pay interest on the money they borrow!

MORTGAGES

A **mortgage** is a loan that helps someone buy a property, such as a house or a warehouse for their business. In many countries, houses are so expensive that most people buy one using a mortgage.

Before agreeing to lend money, the bank studies the borrower's income and debts to make sure that the loan is not too risky. Usually, a home-buyer must pay some of the money for their new home up front. This amount is called a deposit. The rest of the house price is paid by the bank. Then, over many years—perhaps 25 or 30—the home-buyer pays back the loan, plus interest, by making a payment to the bank every month.

SECURING LOANS

If a loan is "secured," the borrower agrees to give the bank a named piece of property if they do not pay back the money as agreed. Mortgages are secured on the building being bought. If the borrower does not pay, the bank can take and sell the building, which is called a foreclosure or repossession. Banks give borrowers warning and advice before taking this step.

OUT OF CURIOSITY

More than 2,000 years ago, ancient Roman lawmakers set out the process for agreeing a loan, including how it was secured.

🏠 LOTS OF LOANS

Common loans include car loans, which help people to buy a car, and personal loans, which help someone meet an unexpected cost or to make home improvements. Car loans are secured on the car. Personal loans are often **unsecured**, so the borrower must pay higher interest and pass extra checks by the bank.

🏠 ISLAMIC LOANS

Islamic banks give loans in a way that keeps to the beliefs of Islam. The work of Islamic banks is based on the belief that money does not have any value in itself, so no one should make money from money. This means that Islamic banks do not charge interest. If someone takes out an Islamic mortgage, they jointly buy the house with the bank, then gradually pay back the bank its share, plus a little extra for the service.

HOW MONEY MOVES

Coins, notes, and electronic money are constantly on the move.
They pass from bank account to bank account—and from
mints to banks to you! But how do they move?

BANKNOTES ARE CARRIED IN BOXES
THAT SPRAY THE NOTES WITH DYE IF
THE BOXES ARE FORCED OPEN RATHER
THAN UNLOCKED WITH A CODE.

CASH INTO CIRCULATION

After a government's banknote printers and mints have made
banknotes and coins, they need to be put into circulation,
which means they go into use, passing from hand to hand.
This is where banks come in! Using electronic money, banks
buy notes and coins from the government's central bank or—
usually—a cash distribution office agreed by the central bank.

Using security vehicles protected by bulletproof glass and thick
metal, notes and coins are taken from distribution offices to
bank branches and automated teller machines (ATMs), also
known as cash machines. When people withdraw money in
cash, the new money goes into circulation!

OUT OF CURIOSITY

**The country that puts
the most banknotes into
circulation is the United
States. In most years, the
Bureau of Engraving and
Printing prints over $200
billion in banknotes.**

CASH OUT OF CIRCULATION

NOTES ARE TAKEN OUT OF CIRCULATION IF THEY SHOW ANY OF THESE TYPES OF DAMAGE.

Banks cannot store large amounts of coins and notes. They also cannot earn interest on them, since they cannot be loaned or used to buy investments. So when banks want to bank their own cash, they sell it back to a cash distribution office and get paid in electronic money. The office works with the mint and banknote printers to remove old or damaged notes and coins, then put the rest back into circulation.

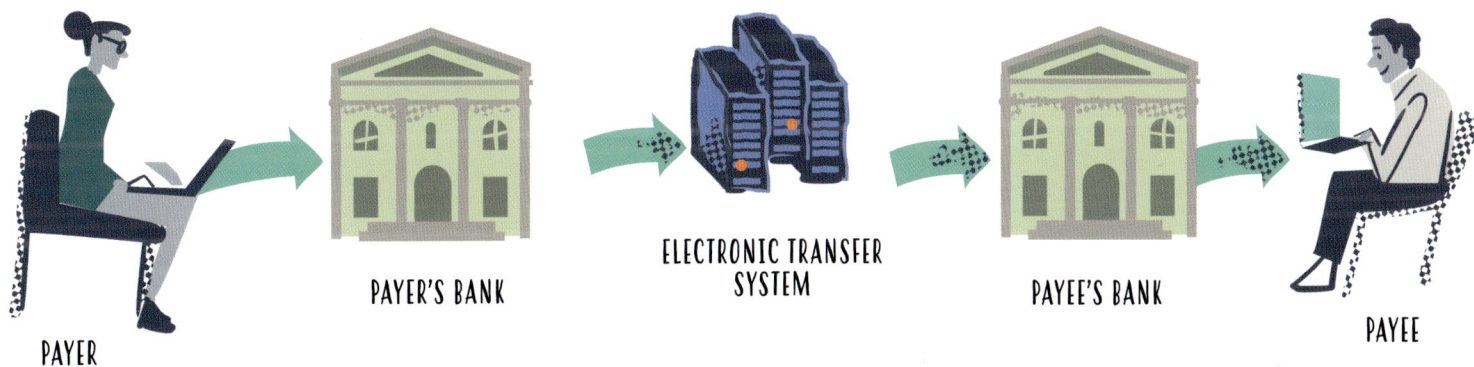

WORN INK

TAPE OR STAPLES

TEARS

DYE FROM A CASH BOX

MISSING PIECES

GRAFFITI

HOLES

HEAT OR WATER DAMAGE

PAYER

PAYER'S BANK

ELECTRONIC TRANSFER SYSTEM

PAYEE'S BANK

PAYEE

MOVING ELECTRONIC MONEY

Usually, when someone pays a bill or an employer pays their workers, no notes and coins move from place to place. Figures on computer screens change! One bank account gets a lower balance, while another gets a higher balance. This is done using electronic transfer systems, which are national or international computer systems.

Often, these systems do not work instantly. They add up all transactions made during the day, then move the total owed by one bank to another at the end of every day. The computer system changes the electronic balances of the sending and receiving banks. Each bank changes the electronic balances of its customers.

DIFFERENT BANKS

Some banks are a little different! They work on different principles from most retail banks. Some don't set out to make a profit. Others make a profit while also trying to make the world a better place.

CREDIT UNIONS

A credit union is a bank that is owned by the people who have deposited money. Most unions are in communities where people have low incomes, so they cannot get a loan from an ordinary bank. Members of a credit union share their savings to lend to one another, at low interest rates. They also share any profits. Small credit unions are run by unpaid volunteers. Big credit unions have thousands of members and paid staff.

? OUT OF CURIOSITY
There are more than 86,000 credit unions, with 90 percent of them in Africa and Asia.

ETHICAL BANKS

An ethical bank invests money and makes loans only in ways that do not cause harm. Ethical banks do not work with companies that mine **fossil fuels** or make cigarettes or weapons. Some also invest in projects that do good, such as tree-planting. Like ordinary retail banks, most ethical banks make a profit.

MICROCREDIT ORGANIZATIONS

Microcredit organizations give small, unsecured loans to people who do not have enough income to be lent money by retail banks. The loans can be spent by a farmer on more seeds or by a store-owner on more goods, which can help people to work their way out of poverty. Some microcredit organizations are funded by charities so they charge low or no interest.

WORLD BANK

The World Bank lends money to the governments of less-wealthy countries for projects that reduce poverty, improve healthcare and education, and work against climate change. The bank is owned by 188 of the world's governments. Wealthier member countries give money so the bank can make low-interest loans, no-interest loans, and **donations**.

THE WORLD BANK LENDS MONEY TO BUILD WIND FARMS. THESE ARE A SOURCE OF ENERGY THAT DOES NOT CAUSE POLLUTION AND WILL NEVER RUN OUT.

BANK ACCOUNT SAFETY

It is important to keep your bank card safe and to keep secret the details of your bank account and payment cards. Don't let someone else use them to get rich quick!

STAYING SECRET

Never let anyone—apart from a trusted adult—know your bank account number, payment card number, **personal identification number (PIN)**, or password, since these could be used to take money from your account. A PIN is a secret number that you type in when paying with a card or getting money from an ATM. A password is typed in when accessing your bank account on a bank's website.

SETTING PASSWORDS

Never use the same password for different accounts. Try to think up passwords that no person or computer could guess. For example, do not use whole words or number sequences, such as 1234. Do use a mix of capital and small letters, numbers, and symbols.

Try creating passwords from easy-to-remember phrases. For example, "My 10-year-old friend Billy loves lollipops!" becomes "M10-y-ofBll!"

PHISHING

Tricking someone into giving away their bank account information is called phishing. A common method is to phone or email, pretending to be from a bank. The criminal then asks for bank account details. Remember that a genuine bank or business will never contact you then ask for your information.

Phishers may also send emails containing links that, if clicked, install programs called malware on your phone or computer. Malware can steal passwords when you type them.

OUT OF CURIOSITY

There are over 1.4 million phishing websites, which pretend to be online stores or other businesses. Before typing in your bank information on a website, search for reviews of the site using its exact address.

KEEP WATCH

Keep a watch on your bank cards and account balance. If you lose your card or see a strange payment from your bank account, call your bank immediately. The bank will prevent more money being withdrawn.

CHAPTER 3

GOVERNMENTS AND MONEY

A key job for every government is to manage the country's money. Managing this money is part of managing the country's whole **economy**. The economy is all about how a country's people are making money, spending money, and sharing money. It is also about how they make, buy, and share all the things that money can buy, including goods—from cucumbers to cars—and services, such as hospitals and schools.

In this chapter, let's find out what makes a strong economy. We'll look at the ways that governments try to keep everything running smoothly. We'll also discover some of the things that can go wrong, so you'll know what people mean next time you hear the words "inflation" or "**recession**"!

MANAGING THE MONEY

What do governments want to achieve when they're managing the country's money? And what can a government do if it isn't achieving what it wants? The problems and solutions are complicated, which is why governments don't always get it right …

WHAT DO GOVERNMENTS WANT?

Governments want a strong economy. So does everyone who lives in every country! But what is a strong economy? Does it just mean that there is lots of money in the country? It does mean that, plus a few more things that help everyone feel the benefit of that money. If an economy is strong, you can say these things about it:

- There are plenty of jobs, so most working-age adults are earning money.
- Fewer and fewer people are living in poverty.
- The economy is growing, which means that there is a rise in the number or quality of goods and services the country is producing. This might mean that the country is making more cars or that it is improving its hotels so they cost more to stay in!
- The value of each money unit—such as a dollar or pound—stays about the same, so it can buy the same amount of goods today as it did last year.

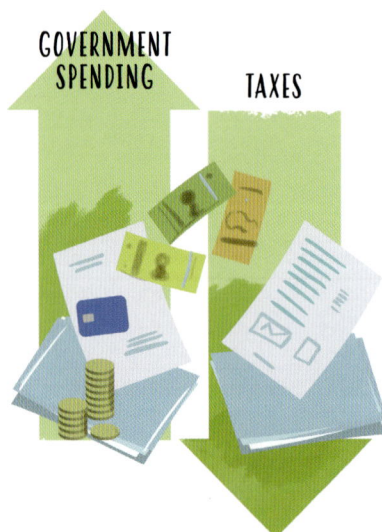

MAKE CHANGES!

A key way for a government to help the economy is by changing its taxes and spending. Tax is the money that governments take from people and businesses to pay for their spending on services such as schools.

To boost an economy that is not growing, a government can take less tax but spend more, for example on building new schools. This creates jobs in school-building and also makes people wealthier, so they will spend more money on goods and services, which creates more jobs!

GOVERNMENT SPENDING

TAXES

INCREASING SPENDING BUT REDUCING TAXES IS A WAY TO GROW AN ECONOMY.

BORROW MONEY!

When governments spend more money than they are taking in tax, they must usually borrow money! This may happen when trying to boost the economy or because of a war or natural disaster. The amount that a government borrows in a year is called the budget deficit. The total amount a government owes is the national debt.

Usually, governments borrow by selling bonds to banks and other financial institutions, such as insurance companies. A bond is for a certain amount of money, interest, and time. For example, $10,000 is borrowed, with 10 percent interest paid every year, and it must be repaid after 10 years. Countries also borrow from each other and from international organizations such as the World Bank (see page 43). If a government borrows a lot, it will be paying too much interest for many years. However, if it manages to boost the economy, it will get more money in tax in the long term!

OUT OF CURIOSITY

One of the wealthiest countries has one of the largest national debts: the Japanese government owes over 1 quadrillion Japanese yen (more than US $8 trillion).

TALK TO THE BANK!

Governments can also help the economy by making the country's **money supply** bigger or smaller. The money supply is all the money in circulation. To do this, a government must talk to its central bank (see page 64).

TAKING TAXES

To pay for all its spending, a government needs money! It gets this money through taking taxes, which are charges paid by people and businesses. Taxes are compulsory, which means you don't get any choice about paying them—you just pay up!

INCOME TAX

Nearly all governments charge income tax. This means that workers pay a percentage of their income, which is the money they earn. Businesses also pay tax on their incomes. In most countries, the more a person earns, the higher the percentage they pay in income tax, which helps to make taxation fairer. Usually, a person with a low income does not have to pay anything.

TAXES, TAXES, TAXES

Countries, as well as cities and regions, can charge other types of taxes. The most common are:

Sales taxes are a percentage of the price of many goods bought in stores. In some countries, the marked price of an item includes sales tax, while in others, the tax is added at the cash register.

Property taxes are usually a percentage of the value of a home or other building, either charged every year or when the property is bought.

Inheritance taxes are a percentage of money passed on by a relative when they die.

Taxes called tariffs are taken when goods enter or leave a country.

?

OUT OF CURIOSITY

Taxes have been collected since at least 5,000 years ago, when the rulers of ancient Egypt took around 20 percent of each grain harvest.

TAX HAVENS

Tax havens are countries or territories that charge little or no income tax. They attract wealthy people and businesses who want a haven—"safe place"—from income tax. However, the governments of these countries often charge a lot in other taxes, including sales taxes, tariffs, and airport taxes, paid when people fly in and out.

HIGH TAX!

Many European countries—particularly Denmark, France, and Sweden—have high taxes. The governments of these countries give lots of services, including healthcare and childcare, at low cost or "free." Since these services are paid for by taxation rather than when using them, people with low incomes can afford them more easily.

SOME TAX HAVENS, SUCH AS THE BAHAMAS, ARE BEAUTIFUL ISLANDS THAT ATTRACT TOURISTS. THE TOURISTS BRING MONEY INTO THE ECONOMY AND PAY HIGH SALES AND AIRPORT TAXES.

SPENDING MONEY

What do governments do with the taxes they collect? They spend the money on public services, which are facilities and activities that everyone can use or enjoy. Many governments also spend money on welfare payments to their own citizens and support for other countries.

SUPER SERVICES

Most governments spend the largest chunk of the country's money on public services. Not all governments spend on the same services, since some pay in full for services such as healthcare, but others—such as the United States—do not. These are the most common public services:

Healthcare including hospitals, doctors, nurses, and medical supplies.

Education for school-age children, possibly also for preschoolers, college students, and adults.

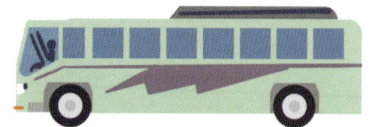

Emergency services, including fire, rescue, and ambulances.

Protecting the environment, including controlling pollution and caring for national parks.

Sports and culture facilities, such as basketball courts and museums.

Housing, roads, water supplies, street lighting, and public transportation.

Soldiers, planes, warships, and tanks.

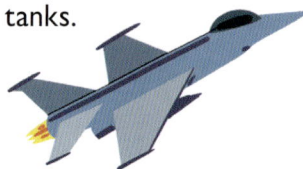

Government work, including lawmakers and office staff.

Police forces, law courts, and prisons.

WONDERFUL WELFARE

Welfare, also known as social protection, is how governments try to make sure that everyone in the country has enough money to meet their basic needs. Countries in Europe, North America, East Asia, and Australasia usually offer the most social protection.

Governments may make welfare payments to people who are unemployed, paid low wages, or unable to work because they are sick, disabled—or have just had a baby. Many governments pay **pensions**, which is money regularly given to people when they retire, usually a portion of the taxes they have paid throughout their working lives!

OVERSEAS AID

Many governments send money to other countries when they suffer a disaster such as an earthquake. Governments also give money for long-term projects in other countries, such as building roads or schools. An extra benefit to this kindness is creating a friendly relationship with another country, which can result in more trade—and money!

OUT OF CURIOSITY

Covering 65,000 sq m (700,000 sq ft), the National Museum of China is the biggest government-funded museum that is free for all visitors.

ECONOMIC SYSTEMS

An economic system is the way that a government organizes and shares the country's resources—such as land and fuel—as well as the production of its services and goods. There are three main types of economic systems: planned, free market, and mixed.

PLANNED ECONOMIES

In this type of economy, the government controls all the country's resources and makes all decisions about the production of goods and services. Factories and farms are run by the government. The aim of a planned economy is for everyone to have an equal share in the country's resources—and the money made from them. In practice, planned economies are difficult to run smoothly because they are so huge.

During the 20th century, many **Communist** countries, particularly in Asia and eastern Europe, had planned economies. Today, the only completely planned economy is North Korea's.

OUT OF CURIOSITY

One of the world's biggest economies, China was a planned economy from 1949 to 1978, but today it has many privately owned businesses.

FREE MARKET ECONOMIES

In a free market economy, land and resources are privately owned, by individual people and businesses. Each business makes all its own decisions, free from government control. A business's decisions are based only on the market: the laws of supply (what goods are for sale) and demand (how many people want to buy them).

In fact, no modern country is purely a free market economy. However, the governments of countries such as Singapore and Switzerland take the least control over businesses.

MIXED ECONOMIES

Nearly all countries are mixed economies, with features of both planned and free market economies to different degrees! This means that most businesses make their own decisions, but governments keep some control.

Most governments make regulations (rules) so that businesses behave fairly and safely. They may also give subsidies (payments) to farmers who grow essential food that does not make much profit. Industries that provide essential goods or services—such as delivering mail—may be run by the government.

LOW AND HIGH INCOME

Some countries are wealthier than others. Wealthier countries have a higher income. But this doesn't tell us everything we need to know about a country and its people!

GETTING INTO INCOME

Economists talk about a country's gross national income. This is the total money earned in a year by a country's people and businesses. The countries with the highest gross national incomes are the United States, China, and Japan.

THE UNITED STATES HAS A POPULATION OF AROUND 333 MILLION PEOPLE. KEY SOURCES OF WEALTH ARE TECHNOLOGY, BANKING, AND MAKING GOODS SUCH AS MEDICATIONS AND PLANES.

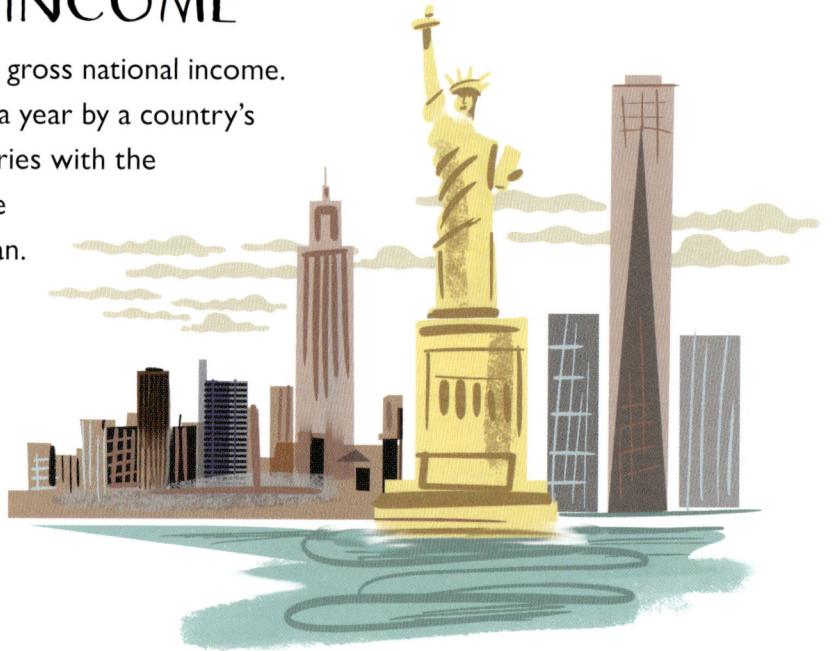

INCOME PER PERSON

Of course, countries with more workers have a better chance of earning more money. To get a clearer idea of the wealth of a country's average person, we can divide its gross national income by the number of people who live there. This makes countries with small populations but very strong economies come out on top, such as Europe's Liechtenstein, Norway, and Luxembourg.

LIECHTENSTEIN HAS A POPULATION OF AROUND 40,000 PEOPLE. MUCH OF ITS WEALTH COMES FROM BANKING AND TOURISM.

DEVELOPED AND DEVELOPING

Economists sometimes call high-income countries "developed" and low-income countries "developing," to give us a picture of what life in these countries is like. "Developed" countries have more people working in offices and factories than on farms. They have good **technology**, transportation, education, and healthcare. Few people live in poverty. In developing countries, the opposite of all these things is true.

WHY LOW OR HIGH?

Why are some countries wealthier than others? Some countries have better natural resources, with good rainfall and land for growing crops, as well as supplies of commodities such as oil. A country's history also plays a big part, including colonization (being taken over) by another country that harmed its development.

All this goes some way toward explaining why low-income countries are more common in particular regions: southern Asia and central Africa. However, today's low-income countries will not stay that way, because their people are planning, working, and inventing …

OUT OF CURIOSITY

Some of the fastest-growing economies belong to today's low-income countries, including Ethiopia and Rwanda.

QATAR, IN WESTERN ASIA, IS A HIGH-INCOME COUNTRY DUE TO ITS OFFSHORE SOURCES OF NATURAL GAS, WHICH CAN BE BURNED AS FUEL.

IMPORTS AND EXPORTS

Every country has imports and exports! Imports are goods made in other countries that are transported into that country to be bought. Exports are the opposite—they are made in that country, then sold around the world.

EXPORTS

Exports can be goods, such as food and books, as well as services such as financial advice and scientific research. Exports are excellent for a country's income, because they bring money into the country from around the world. The world's biggest exporter is China, which has built a powerful economy from selling goods such as machinery and toys (pictured) to other countries.

IMPORTS

All countries import goods and services that are produced more effectively elsewhere. For example, rice is easier to grow in warm, wet regions of India than in Iceland! Movies made in the United States and phones made in South Korea are popular worldwide. Many countries, such as Switzerland, need to import oil, but their exports help pay for it. If countries import too much compared to exports, they will experience a trade deficit.

OUT OF CURIOSITY

New Zealand's biggest export is concentrated milk, which it sells mainly to China, Indonesia, and Thailand.

WHAT'S A TRADE DEFICIT?

A country's net exports is the total value of the country's exports minus the total value of its imports. A net exports figure above zero (more exports than imports) is a trade surplus, which is considered a good thing. A net exports figure below zero (more imports than exports) is a trade deficit, which is considered a less good thing because it means lots of money is flowing out of the country to foreign businesses.

STRIKING A BALANCE

To bring down a trade deficit, governments can support home-grown businesses. They can do this by charging high tariffs on imported goods, making it cheaper for customers to buy goods made in the country. Governments can give subsidies to businesses in their own country, helping them to keep down the cost of their goods so more people buy them. They can also make trade agreements with other countries, where the countries agree to buy particular products from each other.

LOW TARIFFS MEAN THAT THE UNITED KINGDOM IMPORTS ICELAND'S FISH, WHILE ICELAND IMPORTS UK CHEESE.

INFLATION AND DEFLATION

Inflation is when the prices of goods and services are rising. Deflation is when prices are falling. Both inflation and deflation can cause problems. Governments have tools to fix both!

INFLATION

It is normal for the price of goods and services to rise a little, by 2 or 3 percent each year. In fact, this level of inflation can be a sign that an economy is growing. However, inflation becomes a problem when the rise is too fast. Then many people can't afford to buy what they need.

INFLATING INFLATION

High inflation can be caused by a drop in the supply of goods, perhaps because of a shortage of fuel or materials, or because of a war or natural disaster. When there are fewer goods to go around, stores raise their prices. Workers then ask their bosses to increase wages so they can afford what they need. To afford wage increases, bosses put up the prices of the goods they are making, leading to more inflation!

RISING PRICES

RISING WAGES

FIXES FOR INFLATION

In simple terms, inflation is the result of too much money chasing too few goods. To slow inflation, a government can reduce the amount of money in circulation. One method is to cut its spending and raise taxes. This means that people have less money to spend—which slows price rises. A government can also raise interest rates (see page 65).

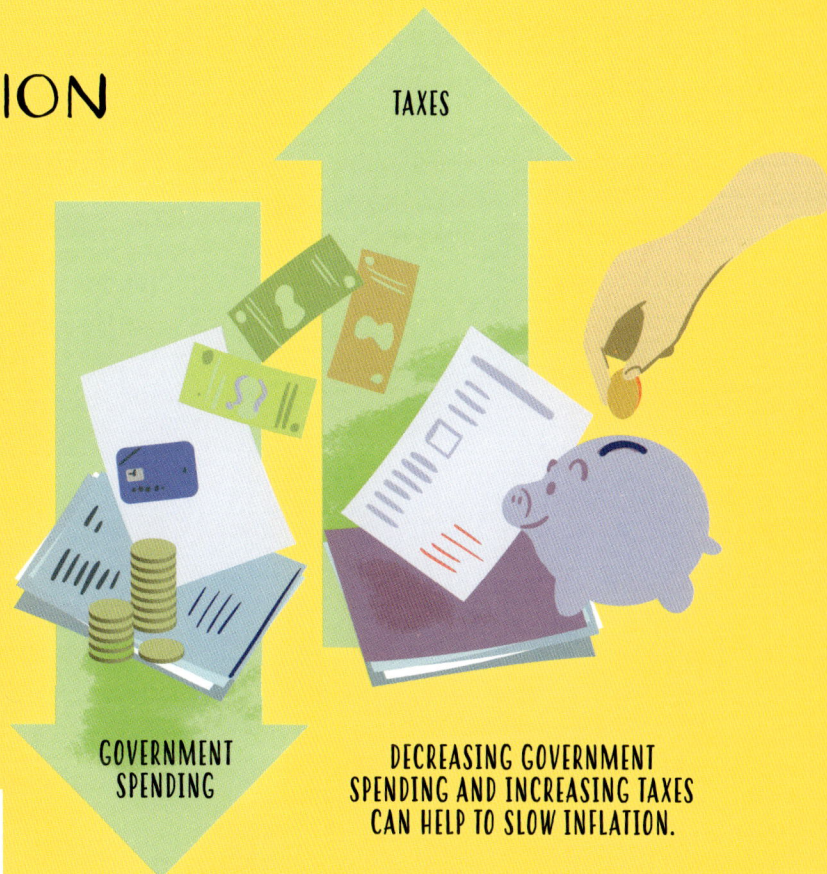

TAXES

GOVERNMENT SPENDING

DECREASING GOVERNMENT SPENDING AND INCREASING TAXES CAN HELP TO SLOW INFLATION.

OUT OF CURIOSITY

The worst inflation was in Hungary in 1946, just after World War II—at one point, prices doubled every 15 hours.

DEFLATION

Deflation happens when people do not have enough money to buy all the goods that are for sale. This makes sellers cut the cost of goods. When businesses can't sell their goods, they also lay off workers (make them redundant: take away their jobs). Unemployed people have less money to spend, so prices fall more. To stop deflation, a government can increase the money in circulation—by raising its spending, cutting taxes, and lowering interest rates (see page 65).

50% OFF!

RECESSION AND DEPRESSION

Governments fear recessions and depressions! A recession is
when a country's economy shrinks for a few months in a row.
A depression is a deeper, longer-lasting downturn.

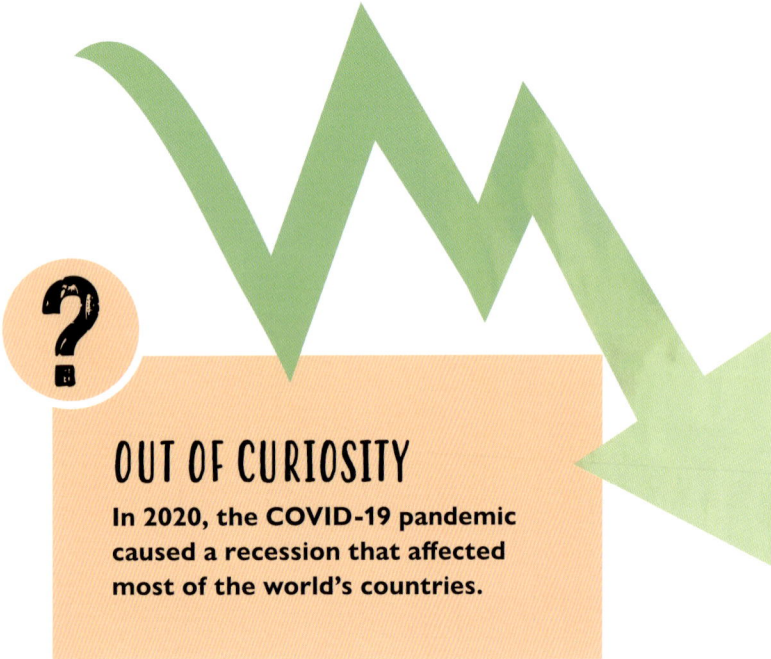

OUT OF CURIOSITY

**In 2020, the COVID-19 pandemic
caused a recession that affected
most of the world's countries.**

WHAT IS A RECESSION?

For economists to agree that a
country is in recession, it must
be producing fewer goods and
services for at least six months.
This is matched with a drop in
the amount of money that people
are spending, as well as a drop in
the number of people with jobs.

WHAT CAUSES RECESSIONS?

Many events can set off a recession.
Here are a few of them:

- A natural disaster, war, or pandemic.

- A financial crisis, such as one caused by too
many people borrowing too much from banks,
then having difficulty paying it back.

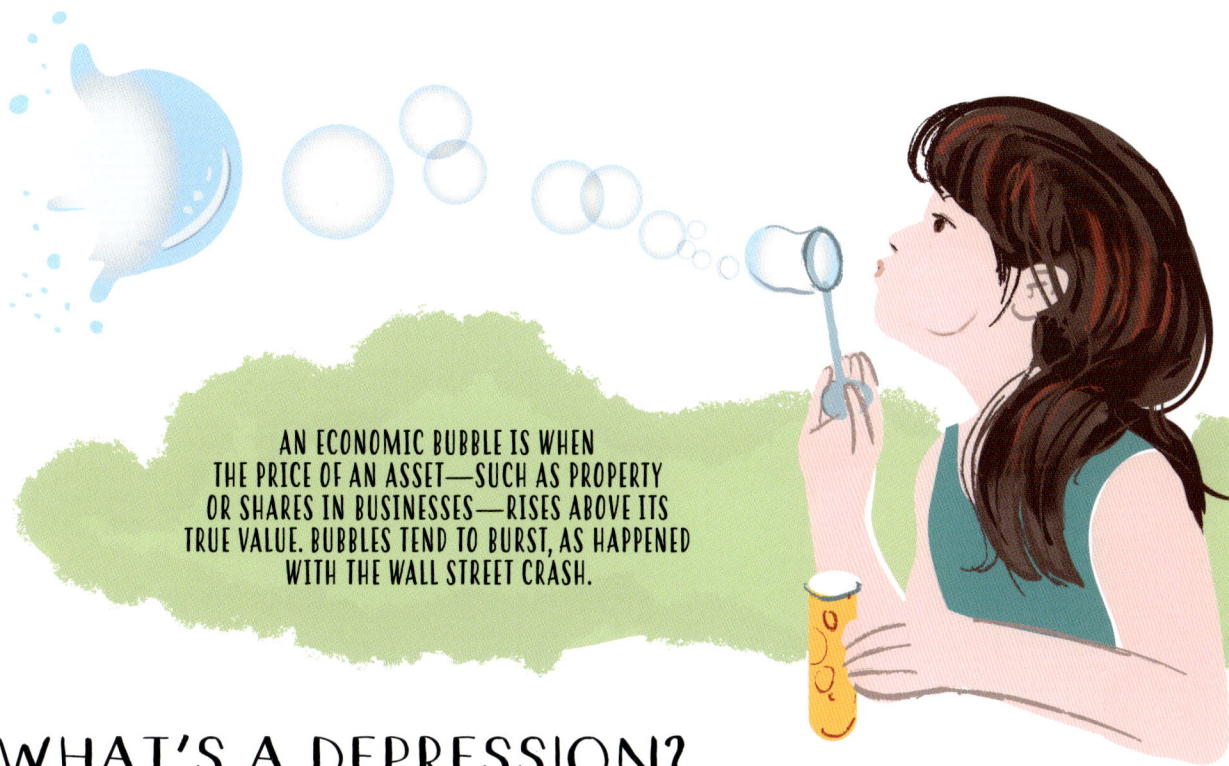

AN ECONOMIC BUBBLE IS WHEN
THE PRICE OF AN ASSET—SUCH AS PROPERTY
OR SHARES IN BUSINESSES—RISES ABOVE ITS
TRUE VALUE. BUBBLES TEND TO BURST, AS HAPPENED
WITH THE WALL STREET CRASH.

WHAT'S A DEPRESSION?

A depression is a deep recession that lasts at least two years. The last true depression was the Great Depression of the 1930s, set off by the United States' Wall Street Crash of 1929.

This famous crash was caused by lots of people rushing to buy shares in companies, causing the price of shares to rise far beyond their true value. Suddenly, everyone lost confidence and sold wildly, wiping out the shares' value, destroying companies and people's savings. The depression spread to many countries around the world.

A drop in other countries wanting to buy a country's products, perhaps caused by a recession in countries that are trading partners.

A rise in the cost of resources, such as oil to use as fuel.

A government or central bank's efforts to slow down inflation (see page 65).

CENTRAL BANKS

Every country or region has a central bank, also called a reserve bank. Unlike a retail bank, a central bank does not look after ordinary people's bank accounts. A central bank oversees the country's money and advises the government about the economy.

MANAGING THE MONEY SUPPLY

A central bank's key job is to control the country's money supply. The money supply is the total money in the country's economy, moving from hand to hand and bank account to account. Central banks make sure the right amount of notes and coins are made. They also oversee how much electronic money is in the country, by changing interest rates.

HOW DO CENTRAL BANKS CHANGE INTEREST RATES?

Interest rates are the percentages that borrowers must pay when they have a mortgage or other loan from a retail bank (see page 30). Central banks do not directly set the interest rates that retail banks charge to their customers—but they do make them change!

Central banks do this by changing the interest rate that retail banks pay on any loans from the central bank. Since retail banks must make a profit, this directly affects the rates that retail banks must charge their customers to borrow money, which also affects the rates of interest that retail banks pay on people's savings.

OUT OF CURIOSITY

The first central bank was the Bank of Sweden, in 1668. The United Kingdom's Bank of England was set up in 1694, while the United States' Federal Reserve began work in 1913.

HELP!

If a retail bank is failing, so that it risks not being able to pay its customers, the central bank can step in. As a last resort, central banks can pay a bank's customers. As well as helping those customers, this keeps everyone's trust in the country's banking system.

WHY CHANGE INTEREST RATES?

When interest rates are raised, people with mortgages and loans (which is many adults) have to pay more to their bank every month, so they have less money to spend. This shrinks the money supply, which can slow inflation (see page 60).

When interest rates are lowered, people pay less to their bank every month, so they have more money to spend. They also earn less interest on their savings, which means they may choose to save less and spend more. All this increases the money in circulation, boosting an economy that is not growing (see page 62).

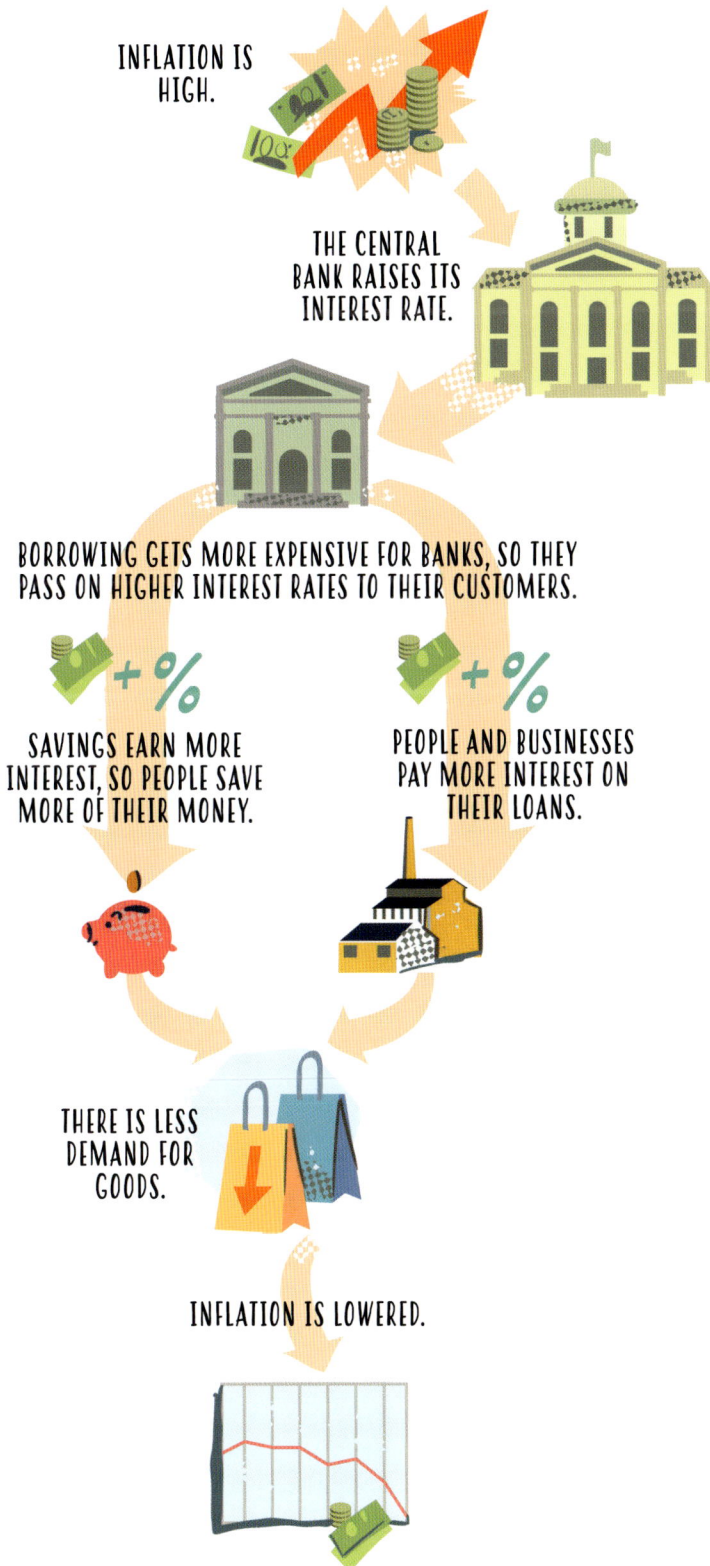

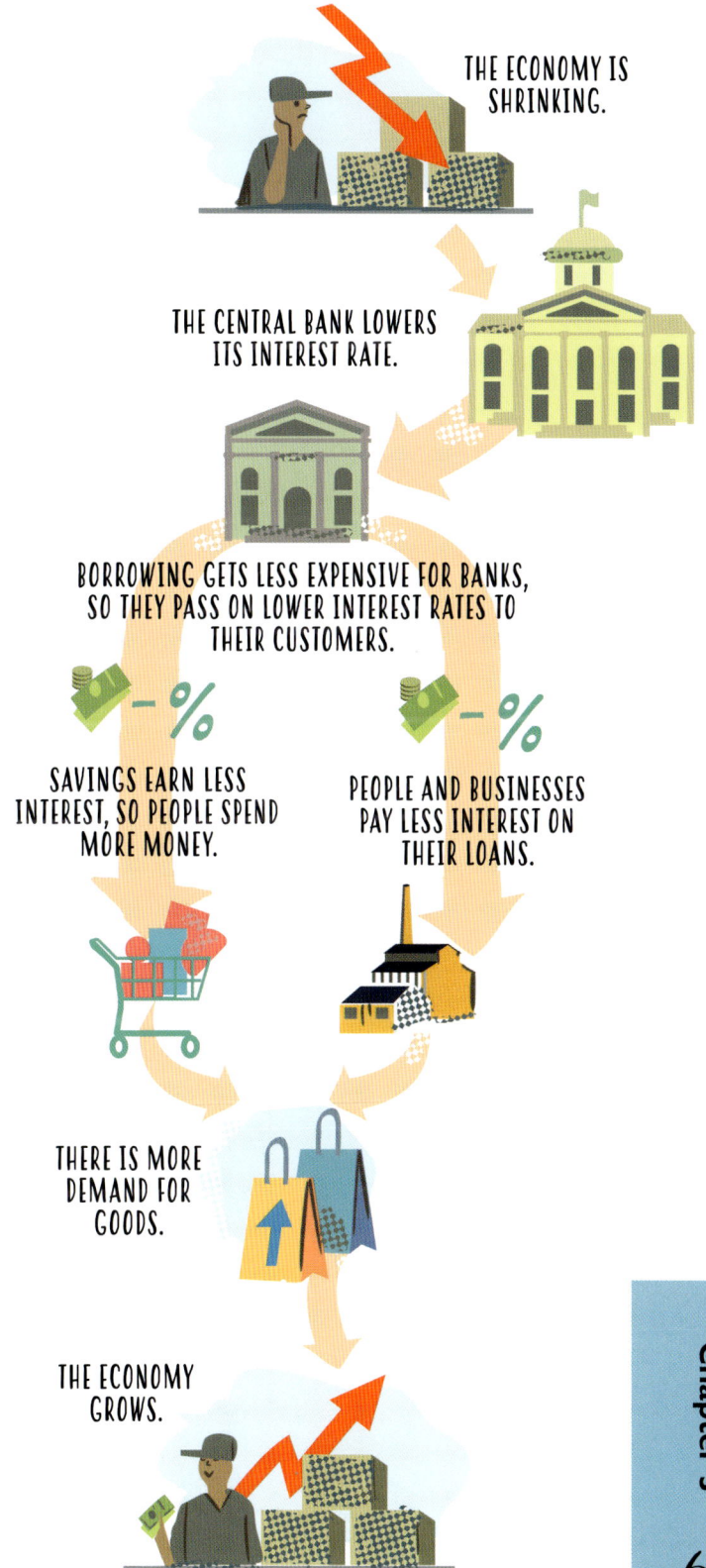

INFLATION IS HIGH.

THE ECONOMY IS SHRINKING.

THE CENTRAL BANK RAISES ITS INTEREST RATE.

THE CENTRAL BANK LOWERS ITS INTEREST RATE.

BORROWING GETS MORE EXPENSIVE FOR BANKS, SO THEY PASS ON HIGHER INTEREST RATES TO THEIR CUSTOMERS.

BORROWING GETS LESS EXPENSIVE FOR BANKS, SO THEY PASS ON LOWER INTEREST RATES TO THEIR CUSTOMERS.

+%

+%

-%

-%

SAVINGS EARN MORE INTEREST, SO PEOPLE SAVE MORE OF THEIR MONEY.

PEOPLE AND BUSINESSES PAY MORE INTEREST ON THEIR LOANS.

SAVINGS EARN LESS INTEREST, SO PEOPLE SPEND MORE MONEY.

PEOPLE AND BUSINESSES PAY LESS INTEREST ON THEIR LOANS.

THERE IS LESS DEMAND FOR GOODS.

THERE IS MORE DEMAND FOR GOODS.

INFLATION IS LOWERED.

THE ECONOMY GROWS.

CHAPTER 4

WORK AND BUSINESS

Since money first developed, working has been how most humans earn it. The way we work has changed over those thousands of years, but the basics have remained the same. We create goods or perform services that meet customers' needs. Today, some say that the world of work is changing so fast that, in the distant future, we may not need to work—or earn money—at all!

In this chapter, we'll find out about the world of work, from contracts to **capital** and farms to factories. We'll discover how businesses produce goods and services, how they persuade customers to buy, and how they make a profit. We'll look at ways that you can put these ideas into practice by starting your own business.

EARNING A LIVING

Most adults have to earn a living! Of course, people work so they can earn money to meet their needs. But there are many other reasons to work, including forming friendships, using skills—and the reward of making or doing something useful.

EARN A SALARY

Most working people have an employer, who pays them a monthly **salary**. When an employee starts a new job, they sign an agreement called a contract with their employer. This agrees the type of work, place of work, the starting salary, and any benefits, such as days of paid vacation or health insurance.

Some employment contracts are for a fixed term, such as a year. Most contracts are permanent, so they state that either employer or employee must give warning of ending the job. An employee may be entitled to an amount of money if their employer lays them off (makes them redundant: ends the job through no fault of the worker).

BE THE BOSS?

Some people are self-employed, which means that they work for themselves. This might be because they started their own business, which employs other people, too. Some self-employed people—including many decorators, photographers, and writers—work alone. Being self-employed brings more freedom but more responsibilities!

CHOOSE A JOB

Many people choose a job that suits their skills, such as drawing, mathematics, or caring for pets. They consider whether they like working in a team or making decisions. They also research the qualifications and number of years' training needed for a job.

WHAT PAYS MORE?

Some jobs are paid better than others! People who work their way up in a business are usually paid more for their experience. People who work as brain surgeons or airline pilots are paid well for their education and responsibility. Some **industries** pay more because the industry itself makes more money. That is why bankers and movie stars earn more than people doing vital jobs such as teaching and fire fighting.

?

OUT OF CURIOSITY

The world's biggest employers include the United States' Walmart stores and McDonald's, as well as China's government-run China Railway.

INDUSTRY SECTORS

Economists often divide businesses into three sectors: primary, secondary, and tertiary, which mean first, second, and third. This is a useful way to group the world of work so we can understand how a country's workforce is employed.

THREE SECTORS

Traditionally, economists use three sectors. The primary sector is collecting or growing **raw materials**. The secondary sector is manufacturing, which is making things from those raw materials. The tertiary sector is carrying out services, which are activities for which somebody will pay.

MORE SECTORS?

In the 21st century, as we worked more with computers, some economists added a fourth sector by separating some industries from the tertiary sector. They separated industries that work with information and ideas, such as information technology (working with computers), education, and blogging.

PRIMARY SECTOR
WORK IN THIS SECTOR INCLUDES FARMING, FISHING, FORESTRY (MANAGING FORESTS), AND MINING OF METALS AND FUELS.

🧹 INDUSTRIES INSIDE SECTORS

Within each sector are lots of different industries. An industry is a group of businesses that make similar **products** or offer similar services, often competing for the same customers. For example, within the secondary sector is the truck-making industry.

OUT OF CURIOSITY

Around the world, more than 15 million people work on fishing boats, which are part of the primary sector.

🧹 WHAT DO SECTORS TELL US?

Economists say that low-income countries (see page 57) have more people working in the primary sector—in fields and mines—than in the secondary or tertiary sectors. In a middle-income country, the workforce is more evenly spread across all three sectors. High-income countries have most people working in the tertiary sector, because many farming and factory jobs have been taken over by machines.

SECONDARY SECTOR

BUSINESSES IN THIS SECTOR MAKE PRODUCTS—FROM COOKIES TO COMPUTERS TO COATS—OR CONSTRUCT BUILDINGS OR BRIDGES.

TERTIARY SECTOR

INDUSTRIES IN THIS SECTOR DO SERVICES FOR OTHER BUSINESSES AND FOR FINAL CUSTOMERS. SERVICES TO BUSINESSES INCLUDE TRANSPORTING AND ADVERTISING PRODUCTS. SERVICES FOR CUSTOMERS INCLUDE TEACHING, NURSING, SERVING FOOD, GIVING LEGAL ADVICE, AND SINGING.

PROFIT AND LOSS

Businesses hope to make a profit—and to avoid a loss! Profit is the money that a business has left after it has met its costs. Businesses usually work out their profit over a particular period, such as a year or three months, known as a quarter.

REVENUE

Revenue is all the money earned by a business by selling its products or services. Revenue is also called gross income or total sales. Let's imagine a business that knits wool sweaters. Its revenue is the total price of all the sweaters sold. If—over a quarter—it sells 1,000 sweaters for $60 each, its revenue is $60,000.

GROSS PROFIT

Not all of a business's revenue is profit. Gross profit is the money left over after paying the direct costs of making products or supplying services. To knit those 1,000 sweaters, our sweater business spent $30,000 on wool and the salaries of the knitters. So the business's gross profit for the quarter was $60,000 minus $30,000—which is $30,000.

OUT OF CURIOSITY

When a customer buys a product such as a sweater, they probably pay sales tax, but that goes to the government so is not part of a sweater business's revenue.

NET PROFIT

A business's gross profit is not its final profit, which is called net profit. Net profit is the gross profit minus operating expenses, which are the costs of running a business day to day. For example, our sweater business paid for two sales staff, **rent** on a store, and electricity. Its operating expenses for the quarter were $20,000. So the business's net profit was $30,000 minus $20,000—which is $10,000.

SUSIE'S SWEATERS

Revenue	$60,000
Production costs	-$30,000
Operating costs	-$20,000
Net profit	= $10,000

POCKET THE PROFIT?

The owner of our sweater business must probably pay some of her $10,000 quarterly profit to the government as income tax. Then, if the owner does not owe money on bank loans, she can pay the rest to herself as a salary or put it in a business savings account. She could also invest it in growing the business by renting a bigger shop.

LOSSES

If a business's revenue, minus its production costs and operating expenses, is less than $0, it has made a loss. If our sweater business had not sold all its sweaters or had bought more expensive wool, it could have made a loss. The owner might have to dip into her savings or ask the bank for a loan to meet her operating expenses.

CAPITAL

Without capital, a business can't function! Capital is the money a business can use to pay for materials, for its day-to-day running, and for future growth. Capital can be profit from the sale of goods and services, but it can also be gained from loans or selling shares.

THE CAPITAL OF A SWEATER BUSINESS INCLUDES AVAILABLE MONEY, UNSOLD SWEATERS, AND UNUSED WOOL.

CALCULATING CAPITAL

It is important for a business to know its capital. The amount of capital in a business shows how easily it can meet its current needs, grow, and face future problems.

When a business is figuring out its capital, it does not just include the money it holds today. It also adds the money it is owed, as well as the value of unsold goods and raw materials that can be sold within the year. From this figure, a business must take away its current liabilities, which is money it owes over the next year. Liabilities include salaries, tax, and repayments of loans.

DEBT CAPITAL

Debt capital is money a business has gained by borrowing, usually from a bank or investors. Debt capital is part of a business's capital, but any repayments due over the next year count as a liability. This form of capital helps businesses expand, but it can become a problem if it creates too large a liability.

EQUITY CAPITAL

Equity capital is gained by selling shares—portions of the business—to investors (see page 122). This does not count as borrowing, since the money does not have to be repaid. Instead, the investor is given regular payments that are a share of the company's profits, small or large depending on the size of the portion they own. Equity capital forms part of a business's capital, but payments to investors are a liability.

CAPITAL ASSETS

When businesses are figuring out how much money they can spend, they usually just include money as capital. However, a business has other types of capital that add value to the business if it is bought in full or sells shares in itself. These are capital assets, including factories, machinery, and **patents**, which are legal rights to be the sole business to profit from an invention.

?

OUT OF CURIOSITY

In 1421, Italian engineer Filippo Brunelleschi was awarded a patent for his invention of a barge with a hoist that lifted marble slabs.

SUPPLY CHAINS

A supply chain is a network of businesses that are involved in making and delivering a product to a customer. Chains often start with the miners, loggers, or farmers who source raw materials. They can end with the delivery person who hands you a product!

A SIMPLE CHAIN

Even the simplest supply chain involves several businesses. The supply chain for a wooden chair starts with a forestry business. It continues with a transportation business, which delivers wood to a wholesaler. A wholesaler is a business that sells materials and products to other businesses, rather than to individual customers, who are called **consumers**. Wholesalers sell in larger quantities and at lower prices.

After buying and carving wood, a carpentry business pays another transportation business to deliver the finished chair to a **retailer**, which is a store that sells goods to consumers.

OUT OF CURIOSITY

In 1992, Book Stacks Unlimited became one of the first online retailers. It was a website that sold books to consumers.

THE RETAIL PRICE OF A WOODEN CHAIR TAKES INTO ACCOUNT THE COSTS AND PROFITS OF EVERY BUSINESS ITS WOOD PASSES THROUGH.

A COMPLEX CHAIN

For a complex product, such as a phone, the supply chain includes many more businesses, because it requires several materials, including plastics, metals, and glass. In addition, a large technology business may employ other businesses to carry out research, marketing (see page 78), advertising, and customer service (help given to people who buy a product).

GETTING IT RIGHT

In large businesses, people are employed to watch over supply chains. They make sure that materials and products arrive at the right time. They watch costs of all stages so that a consumer can afford the end product. They create options so that a problem with one material does not stop the whole process.

RESPONSIBILITY

Many large businesses have supply chains that stretch across the world. These businesses have a responsibility to make sure that everyone in the chain, from coffee growers to T-shirt sewers, is paid fairly and has a safe workplace. Businesses must ensure that materials are sourced without polluting—and **sustainably**, so for every tree cut down a new one is planted.

MARKETING

Marketing is attracting customers to a product or service. Most large businesses employ marketers. The first step for a marketer is to figure out the possible customers for a product or service, known as its market.

MARKET RESEARCH

Market research is finding out what possible customers think of a new product or service. It allows a business to find out who is most likely to buy—the target market—as well as how much they might pay and where they might buy. Market researchers ask people questions, perhaps in stores or over the phone, and they monitor what people buy in stores and online.

THE FOUR PS

Market research helps a marketing team to figure out the four Ps:

- Product: Marketers figure out the final details of a product's design, quality, and branding (see page 80).

- Price: Marketers help set a price for each product, since they know that their target market wants a low-cost washing powder or will pay a month's salary for a diamond necklace!

- Place: They make sure that products get to where people will buy them, from online stores to boutiques to supermarkets.

- Promotion: The marketing team decides how to promote (encourage people to buy) a product, through advertising, social media, and sales promotions such as free samples, competitions, and money-off coupons.

OUT OF CURIOSITY

At least 5,000 years ago, ancient Egyptians were creating adverts on posters made of paper-like papyrus.

📢 ADVERTISING

Small businesses often create their own advertising, but large ones pay an advertising business. First, they tell the advertisers what to emphasize in the advertising campaign—for example, that a theme park is fun and safe.

Campaigns try to make the target market associate a product with these positive qualities, often using strong images and **slogans**, which are short, easily remembered phrases. Campaigns may run on TV, websites, and large boards called billboards, or through the sponsorship of events such as soccer matches.

📢 SOCIAL MEDIA

Social media—such as YouTube and Instagram—is used by marketers to talk directly to their target market by placing advertising on material they watch and share. Marketers may create a viral marketing campaign, which encourages consumers to share information about a product or service. Viral campaigns may be based on a joke, meme, or competition.

⭐ BRANDING ⭐

Branding helps people to tell a business apart from other businesses. Branding can be based on a name, slogan, design, or even a feeling. It is really useful when many products—such as sports shoes—are nearly identical, since branding makes customers choose one product over another!

⭐ ABOUT THE LOOK

Branding is often created through the look of a product or its packaging, which stays the same year after year. Most products or packaging are marked with the business's name, which is often styled into a logo—a bold symbol made up of text and images.

?

OUT OF CURIOSITY

Trademarks began with the symbols stamped on swords by ancient Roman blacksmiths, so people would recognize their products.

Sometimes, a logo does not contain words but is a design or pattern that is easily recognized, such as wiggles, stripes, or stylized animals or objects. Logos, designs, and even shapes of packaging can be trademarked, which means they cannot legally be used by any other business.

★ MORE THAN LOOK

A brand can be based not on the look of a business's products but on the business's values, personality, or relationship with its customers. For example, a car business can base its brand on being reliable. A retail bank can be caring. A fast-food chain can be family-friendly.

A business will go to great lengths to protect this branding since it can only be gained and kept through watching the quality of its products, the feelings given by its advertising, and by customers who find that the brand has met their expectations.

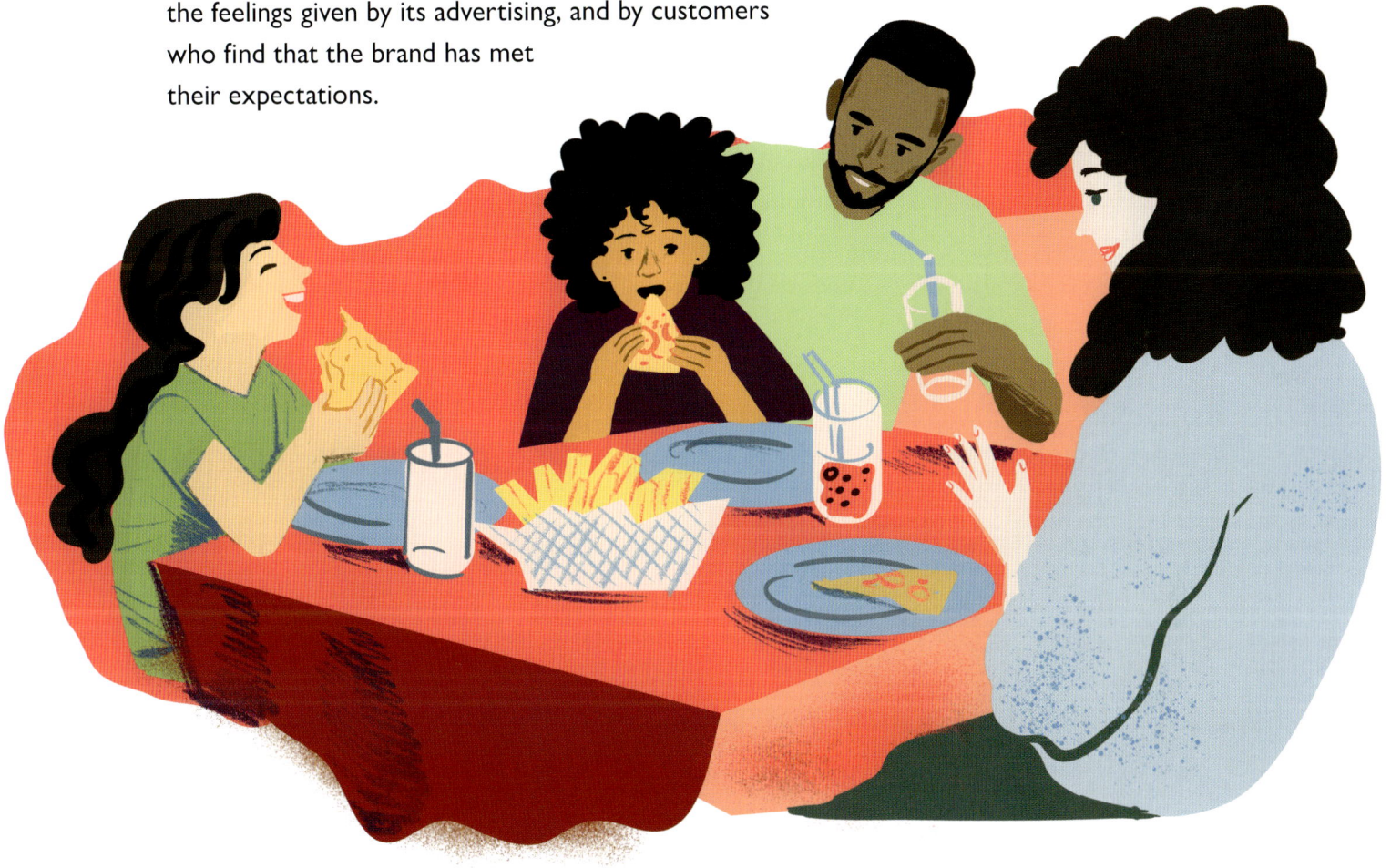

★ INTANGIBLE ASSET

Successful branding is so valuable that it can be listed among a business's capital assets (see page 75). Along with assets such as patents, a brand is known as an intangible (not possible to touch) asset. It is an asset because it earns money—and can be bought and sold for money.

CHANGING WORKPLACE

The workplace is changing, as computers and robots take over jobs that could once be done only by people. What does this mean for the future of work—and even for the future of money?

WHAT IS ARTIFICIAL INTELLIGENCE?

Artificial intelligence (AI) is computer programs that let computers make complex decisions, so that they appear to "think" like humans. All programs give computers sets of instructions. The instructions in an AI program instruct computers on making choices, based on the results of past choices and the likelihood of getting the best result.

AI programs also instruct computers to check lots of data, or information, before coming to a decision. For example, if an AI program teaches a farming robot to kill weeds, it includes lots of photos of weeds.

1789
STEAM-POWERED COTTON-WEAVING MACHINES TAKE OVER FROM HUMAN WEAVERS IN SOME OF THE EARLIEST FACTORIES.

1889
THE FIRST OIL-POWERED TRACTORS START WORK ON FARMS.

OUT OF CURIOSITY

The first mobile robot with basic AI, named Shakey, was completed in 1972.

AI CHANGES WORK

Robots with AI programming are already doing tiring, repetitive work in many factories, warehouses, and farms. Computers with AI programs are predicting the weather, checking people's bank accounts for signs of fraud, and carrying out web searches.

As AI programs get smarter—and even start to program themselves—people wonder if AI-equipped computers and robots will take over more jobs, perhaps all of them!

UNIVERSAL BASIC INCOME

What would happen if computers and robots did all the work? How would humans get money to meet our needs? Some people think the answer might be a universal basic income, which means that everyone is paid the same salary for not working. Yet what about all the other things that humans get from work, such as the pleasure of doing something useful? Humans are very adaptable, so we'll probably think of something!

PAST CHANGES

Over the last few hundred years, new inventions have changed workplaces again and again. With every change, some people lost their jobs to the new machines. However, at the same time, new jobs developed, some of them in overseeing and creating new machines!

1945
THE EARLIEST COMPUTERS BEGIN TO TRANSFORM OFFICE WORK.

1990
THE FIRST AI SEARCH ENGINE, NAMED ARCHIE, SEARCHES THE INTERNET.

START A BUSINESS

With an adult's permission and help, you are never too young to start a small business. You can use your business's profits to save up for a special treat—or give the profits to a charity that you care about.

SET UP A STAND

Sell homemade lemonade, cookies, or cakes from a stand you can set up outside your home. You will need capital to buy ingredients, such as lemons, sugar, flour, chocolate, and eggs. Your capital could come from your savings or a loan by an adult. Make sure you set a price for your products that covers your costs, loan repayments, and some profit.

CREATE A COMIC

Create a comic with a group of friends! Think carefully about the supply chain that will get your comic produced and delivered to customers: You will need editors, artists, writers, printers, delivery people, and salespeople, as well as paper, pens, staples, and a photocopier or printer.

MAKE BEAUTY PRODUCTS

If you can buy the raw materials from an online or local craft store, you could start a secondary-sector industry by making beauty products such as soaps, bath bombs, and lipsalves. Beauty products often have very strong branding, so spend time thinking about how to name and package your products.

PROVIDE A SERVICE

Join the tertiary sector by providing a service to family and friends. Your service should be closely linked to your skills—for example, you could offer gardening, car-washing, or guitar lessons. It can be difficult to set a price on services because the largest cost is time, so conduct market research by asking your target market how much they are willing to pay.

OUT OF CURIOSITY

A profit margin of 10 percent or more is considered good. This means that, from each $100 of revenue, $10 or more should be profit.

CHAPTER 5

SPENDING

Having money to spend gives us opportunities and possibilities, but it also presents us with difficult decisions. The first of those decisions is picking what is essential spending and what is not. The second is about how to spend money sensibly and safely, by finding good-value items from reliable stores. The third decision is about whether we can use our spending choices to help charities or to reward businesses that protect their workers, animals, and the environment.

In this chapter, we'll look at the difference between needs—what we must have to survive, such as food and shelter—and wants, which might be fun to buy if we have money to spare. We'll also examine how our spending can be influenced by friends, advertising, and sales promotions.

THE COST OF LIVING

You've probably heard adults talking about the cost of living. It is the amount that someone must spend to cover basic needs such as housing, food, and heating. The cost of living is different in different places and at different times.

DIFFICULT TO MEASURE

It is difficult to put an exact figure on the cost of living because different people have different needs and expectations. However, financial organizations create cost-of-living indexes, which track the changing costs of the same items across countries.

Indexes help us measure an "average" cost of living in comparison with an average salary to judge how well people in a particular place can afford to live. In general, the cost of living rises a little year after year due to inflation. If inflation rises more quickly than salaries, people find **budgeting** more difficult.

WHERE IS MOST EXPENSIVE?

Cost-of-living indexes tell us that some countries are more expensive than others. Europe's Switzerland has one of the highest costs of living. However, that does not mean that Swiss people can afford less, as salaries are higher in Switzerland than in surrounding countries.

SWITZERLAND'S LARGEST CITY, ZÜRICH HAS ONE OF THE WORLD'S HIGHEST COSTS OF LIVING.

Cities often have a higher cost of living than the countryside, since housing—which is the biggest cost for most adults—is more expensive because of high demand and limited space. However, other costs—such as food and childcare—may be the same or lower than in the countryside as there is more competition between providers, which keeps prices down.

WHAT ARE THE COSTS OF LIVING?

Most adults have to—or want to—spend money on some or all of these things:

HOUSING, INCLUDING RENT OR MORTGAGE REPAYMENTS

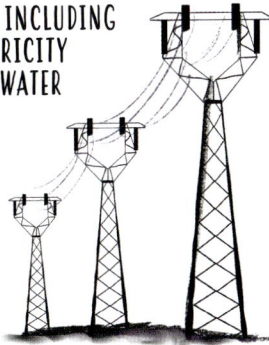

UTILITIES, INCLUDING ELECTRICITY AND WATER

FOOD AND DRINK

CHILDCARE

TRANSPORTATION

TAXES

EDUCATION

ENTERTAINMENT

HEALTHCARE

OUT OF CURIOSITY

The city of Hong Kong, in China, has one of the highest costs of living, partly because of rents, which take more than 40 percent of the average Hongkonger's salary.

CLOTHING

WHAT'S IN A PRICE?

You're standing in a store, ready to pay for a new purchase!
What do you need to know about the price of your purchase?
And what should you do with the receipt?

WHO GETS WHAT?

When you buy a product in a store, have you ever wondered how much of the money goes to the manufacturer or the store? The exact answer depends on taxes and the type of product. Yet, to get an idea, let's take a look at the different costs that make up the final retail cost of a T-shirt:

10%
WAREHOUSING

This includes the cost of storing the T-shirt by both the wholesaler (who bought from the manufacturer; see page 76) and the retailer (who bought from the wholesaler and sells to you).

60% or more
MARK-UP

Before the wholesaler sells the T-shirt to the retailer, they "mark up" its price so they can make a profit on top of their costs. After buying from the wholesaler, the retailer does the same, so they can pay for expenses such as salespeople—and make a profit. A wholesaler's mark-up may be 15 percent of the final price, while the retailer's may be 45 percent or more. The more luxurious the brand, the higher the retailer's mark-up.

KEEP THE RECEIPT!

Receipts are proof of purchase, so if something you buy is faulty, showing the receipt may help you return it. Many countries have laws that protect a customer's right to return faulty items within a certain time. Different stores also have their own rules, including how long you can wait before returning, whether you can return something that isn't faulty, and whether you can only exchange non-faulty goods or get a refund of your money.

Receipts are also a record of your spending. If you are spending too much, check through your receipts to track your costs. Adults have to keep receipts when they want to claim the items as expenses, if their business pays them back for work-related spending. Depending on an adult's tax situation, they may use receipts for "tax deductible" items (which can be subtracted from income, before figuring out the tax due) to reduce their tax bill.

15%
PRODUCTION
Work that goes into producing a T-shirt includes designing, sewing, marketing, and finance.

5%
MATERIALS
Material costs include the production and transportation of cotton, yarn, and dye.

OUT OF CURIOSITY
In the United Kingdom, no sales tax is paid on children's clothes, but 20 percent of the retail price is paid on adults' clothing.

0–25%
TAX
Depending on where you buy the T-shirt and where it was made, the government may take anything from 0 to more than 25 percent of the final retail price in sales tax and import tariffs.

10%
TRANSPORTATION
The T-shirt has journeyed from the manufacturer to the wholesaler's warehouse, then to the retailer's warehouse, then to the store.

NEED OR WANT?

Whether you're an adult with a salary or a young person with pocket money, it is worth remembering a key rule—try to spend less than your income! To keep your spending down, it's useful to recognize the difference between a need and a want.

WHAT'S A WANT?

A want is anything that's not a need! Wants are things that may improve the quality of your life, which means they may increase your comfort or happiness. Wants include things such as accessories, entertainment, eating in restaurants, and trips. Everyone has wants, because we want to have fun and experience the world!

WHAT'S A NEED?

A need is anything you must have to live, work, and learn safely. Needs include shelter, food, clothing, heating, education, and medical care. If you have to use transportation to get to school or work safely, that also counts as a need. Spending on needs is always essential.

? OUT OF CURIOSITY

More than 80 percent of the world's population has never taken a trip on a plane.

DO YOU REALLY REALLY WANT IT?

Before spending money on a want, take a moment to decide if it will really improve your quality of life. A good question to ask yourself is—a few months from now, will I still be glad I spent money on this?

For example, buying a sweatshirt from an expensive brand—rather than a warm but cheaper one—may not keep on making you happy. You might feel disappointed when the sweatshirt goes out of fashion. However, if you spend money on making a good memory with family or friends, it may be a good investment!

STRIKING A BALANCE

Financial experts advise us to aim for the 50–30–20 rule, if we have enough money to get by. The rule means that (after paying any tax) you spend 50 percent of your income on needs, 30 percent on wants, and the remaining 20 percent on paying off debts or saving for the future.

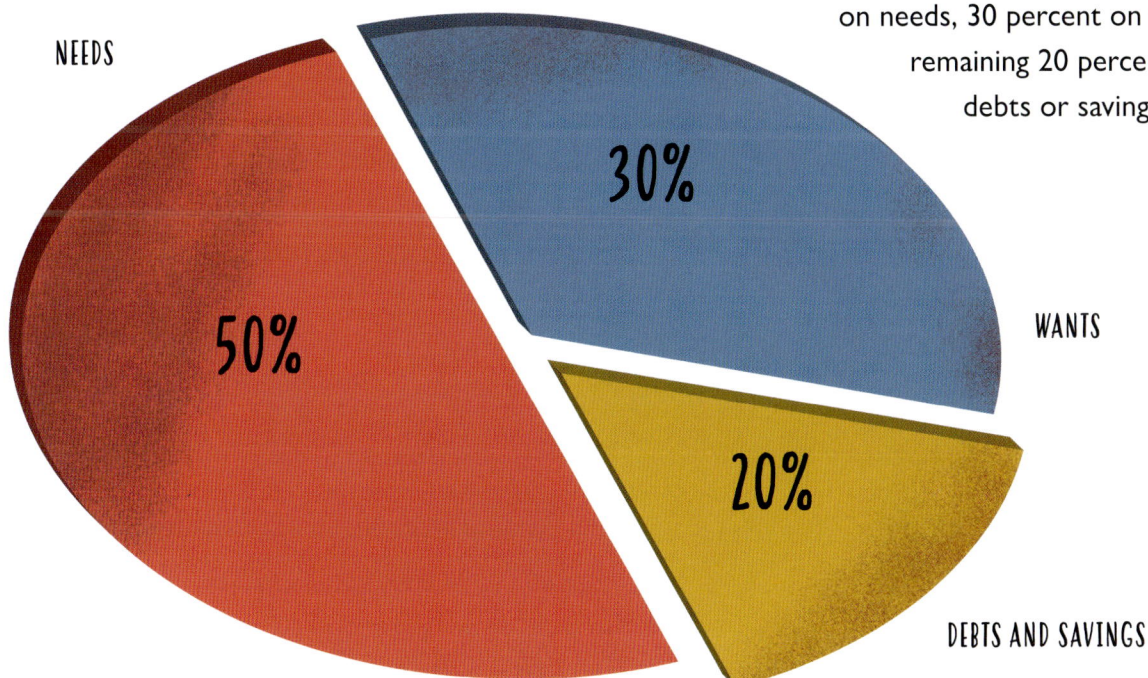

NEEDS

50%

30%

20%

WANTS

DEBTS AND SAVINGS

PEER PRESSURE

Your peers are people of the same age. When your friends or classmates—your peers—make you feel a need to do something, it's called peer pressure. This pressure can encourage you to spend money on things you don't need.

THE ROOTS OF PEER PRESSURE

Since the days of our long-ago ancestors, humans have lived in groups. Fitting in with our group was always key to survival. Today, most of us still feel that need to fit in, particularly with members of our particular "tribe"—our peers. This can make us easily influenced by what our peers are doing, saying, and buying.

UNSPOKEN PRESSURE

When we feel pressure to buy particular items, it is not usually because of any spoken pressure from our peers. It is more likely we notice that everyone in the class has the same expensive brand of backpack or phone or bracelet. This makes us want it, too!

ASK QUESTIONS

When peer pressure makes you think about spending on a want rather than a need, ask yourself a few questions. Is the purchase useful? Is it good value? Will you regret buying it? Then remind yourself that a good friend will never like you more because of anything bought in a store.

OUT OF CURIOSITY

Psychologists have noticed that peer pressure also affects giving to charity—when friends can see what they give, people often give more!

STAY STRONG

Resisting peer pressure can be difficult if you hang out with a group who often spend money on expensive clothes, food, or entertainment. Don't be embarrassed to explain if you want to save rather than spend. Understanding that everyone has different budgets is a key lesson in learning the value of money.

ADVERTISING AWARENESS

Large businesses spend lots of money on advertising that tries to persuade people to buy their products and services. If you don't want to be persuaded to spend money on things you don't really need or want, learn these tricks of the advertising trade!

IN THE MOVIES

Moviemakers earn money not just from people watching their films but from persuading people to buy products. Product placement is when moviemakers are paid by businesses to show characters wearing their watches or driving their cars.

Many children's movies have merchandise tied in with them, including soft toys, games, and clothing that features the characters. After enjoying the movie, many children feel they want to buy.

OUT OF CURIOSITY

One of the earliest movies, 1896's *Laveuses* ("Washerwomen") by the Lumière brothers, featured product placement of Sunlight soap.

BEAUTIFUL PEOPLE

Advertisers want us to believe that buying a certain product or service will make our lives better. Commercials and adverts for clothing and makeup usually feature beautiful models or actors. Subconsciously (without being fully aware of it), we may be persuaded that we will also look perfect if we use the products.

For other products and services, from floor cleaners to hotel chains, advertisers may use more ordinary-looking actors and models—but they nearly always seem happy, popular, or successful!

VALUABLE VLOGGING

Popular social media stars—from professional vloggers to singers and basketball players—are often paid by businesses to use or talk about their products. If you admire the star, you may find yourself admiring the product. The same is true of online gamers and unboxers, who video themselves unwrapping gadgets and toys. Most of them are paid—or given free products—for making the products seem fun!

SMART SHOPPING

Be a smart shopper by considering your spending choices wisely. Look for good deals, but don't let the promise of a deal persuade you to spend more than you can afford.

WAIT FOR A SALE

In a sale, the price of goods may be reduced by 10, 20, or 30 percent. Many clothing stores, particularly those in countries with cold winters and warm summers, have twice-yearly sales to clear out the old season's stock and make room for new items.

It can be worth waiting for sales or even thinking ahead to the winter coat you will need next year. However, don't be persuaded to buy items you don't need, just because they're reduced.

MAKE COMPARISONS

If you need a new high-price item, such as a laptop or bicycle, compare prices between stores. If two stores stock items that are the same quality and price, compare any added benefits, such as free delivery or a warranty. A warranty is a promise by a manufacturer or retailer to repair, refund, or exchange the item if it becomes faulty within a certain time.

?

OUT OF CURIOSITY

In 1908, the first car warranty was offered by the United States' Ford Motor Company. It promised to make repairs for nine months after purchase.

CHECK THE WEIGHT

When buying food and household goods in a supermarket, check not only the prices of similar products but their weight or the number of items each pack contains. A larger, heavier pack may cost more, but it might be better value because of a lower cost per item, gram, or ounce.

WATCH PROMOTIONS

Be aware of the benefits and drawbacks of sales promotions, such as "buy two and get a third one free" or "buy one, get a second one half price." If you need two or more of the same item, these could be good deals. If not, don't be encouraged to spend extra money.

ETHICAL CHOICES

In addition to spending wisely, we can also try to spend ethically. This means that, when we have a choice and enough money, we can buy products that help make the world fairer, kinder, or less polluted.

KINDER TO ANIMALS

Some people choose goods that were produced with methods that do not cause unnecessary suffering to animals. "Free range" meat, eggs, and milk come from animals that were not kept in cramped enclosures all day. "Dolphin safe" tuna was fished in ways that are unlikely to tangle dolphins. Beauty products that were "not tested on animals" often state it on their packaging.

KINDER TO THE PLANET

Food labeled as "organic" has been farmed without using chemicals that can harm wildlife, including bees, birds, and butterflies. Buying food that was grown locally can also be kinder, since less fuel was burned to bring it across the world by plane and truck.

SUSTAINABLE

Choosing products that were sourced sustainably is also kinder to the environment. For example, paper and card that bears the FSC (Forest Stewardship Council) mark were sourced from forests where at least one tree was planted for every tree cut down.

PLASTIC FREE

Plastic packaging causes litter and pollution, because plastic can take many years to break down, is difficult to recycle, and is usually made from **fossil fuels**. When possible, choose products with no packaging, little packaging, recycled-plastic packaging, or packaging made from other materials, including more easily recycled paper, metal, and glass.

FAIR TRADE

Products labelled "fair trade" have a fairer supply chain. These products—including bananas, chocolate, coffee, cotton, sugar, and tea—may cost more than similar products, because the manufacturers have paid a higher (and fairer) price to the growers, who are often in middle- or low-income countries.

OUT OF CURIOSITY

Labeling that advertises ethical production is most common in North America, Europe, and Australasia, but in the rest of the world, some products meet the same standards.

GIVING TO CHARITY

If you have money to spare, giving to charity is a fantastic choice! If you don't have spare cash, you could raise money for charity with an adult's help. Here are some ideas about where to start.

CHOOSING A CHARITY

Start by looking for a charity that helps a cause you care about, such as cat welfare or an illness that has affected family or friends. Find out about charities working in that area, discovering how much impact they make by spending money in ways that make the most difference. Check to see if the charity is officially registered as a charity.

OUT OF CURIOSITY

Despite not being the wealthiest country, Southeast Asia's Myanmar is one of the most charitable—more than 80 percent of its people give to charity regularly.

YOU COULD JOIN A SPONSORED RACE ORGANIZED BY A CHARITY.

🌷 FUNDRAISING

Before you start on a fundraising plan, try asking your chosen charity for branded sponsorship forms, stickers, or collection boxes. Tell everyone about the charity before asking them to donate. Here are a few ideas for fundraising:

- 🪙 Ask family and friends to sponsor you for walking, running, or bicycling a certain distance.

- 🪙 Sell tickets for a party, quiz, movie night, or art show.

- 🪙 With an adult's permission, sell your old clothes, toys, and books.

- 🪙 Give the profits from your own business (see page 84).

🌷 IDEAS ABOUT CHARITY

Most religions teach that charity is a duty for anyone who is able. For Jews, *tzedakah* (which means both fairness and charity) is an obligation to give money, food, or gifts. For Muslims, *zakat* is a central principle of Islam—adults must give 2.5 percent of their income every year.

Many atheists (people who do not believe in God) also see charity as a responsibility, believing that altruism—caring about others more than oneself—should be a guiding principle.

ONLINE SHOPPING SAFETY

More and more people are going online to shop. This makes shopping quick and easy, but it brings the risk of having money taken by fraudsters and **hackers**. Use these tips to stay safe.

🔒 CHECK THE WEBSITE

Some fraudsters create fake websites that look like online stores, so they can steal people's payment details. Try these tips for spotting fake sites:

- A fake website may have poor-quality photos and spelling mistakes.
- A real website will contain information such as the contact details of the business, delivery facts, and returns information.
- Look for customers' reviews of the website by doing an online search using its address. Watch out for the same review being repeated on several review sites.
- Make sure that the website is not pretending to belong to a well-known store by using an address similar to—but slightly different from—the famous store's name.
- Only access sites by doing a search, never by clicking on a link sent in an email.

🔒 CHECK THE CONNECTION

Before paying, look at the icon at the left side of the address bar, which is at the top of your screen. A "closed padlock" or "tune" icon does not mean the website is genuine, but it probably means your connection is secure—so no one else can see the payment details you type. An exclamation mark means that the connection is not secure.

TUNE ICON

CHECKING OUT

When entering your information at a website checkout, only give essentials such as your delivery address and payment information, never anything that would help a criminal figure out your bank account password.

Do not pay by transferring money from your bank account, since that would give a fraudster access to your money—and banks will rarely give customers that money back. Debit cards—and, even better, credit cards (which are only for adults)—are a safer way to pay.

OUT OF CURIOSITY

The world's most commonly used password is also the easiest for hackers to guess: 123456.

CREATING ACCOUNTS

Many retailers suggest that you create an account with them so you can save your delivery and payment card details for next time. This puts you at greater risk from hackers, who could break into the store's computer system to take card details. However, if you do create an account with a genuine store that you use regularly, make sure your password is secure (see page 44), and never use the same password for different stores.

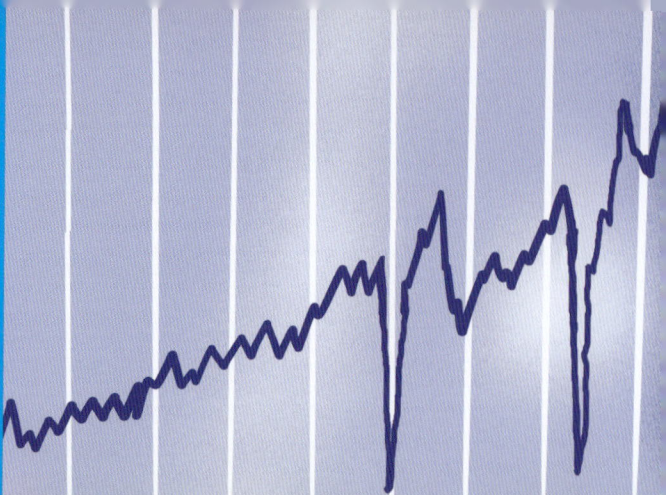

CHAPTER 6
SAVING AND INVESTING

Saving money means not spending all your money as soon as you get it. It means not buying a chocolate bar every week, so that—in a few weeks or months—you can afford to buy a movie ticket or a guitar! Saving money can help you afford more expensive items, plan for the future, and meet your goals. Saving sounds dull, but it opens the door to a world of opportunities.

In this last chapter of the book, we'll get some tips on how to budget and save money. We'll look at a range of options for how to prepare financially for the future, such as pensions and insurance policies. Finally, we'll find out about investments, which are ways of putting money to work, so that, in the future, it might make you a profit.

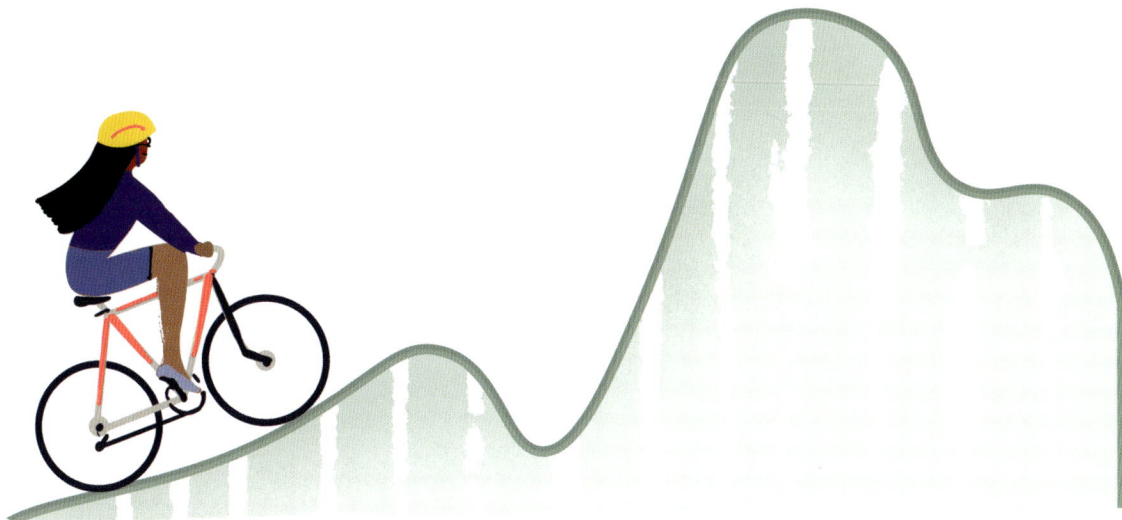

SAFE SAVING

Do you want to buy a skateboard or a new soccer ball, but don't have the cash? You could save up the money by putting a little away each week, until you have enough to meet your goal. But how should you start saving safely?

SHORT-TERM SAVING

To save small amounts of money, a piggy bank or money box is perfect. Keep it in a safe place at home. For larger amounts, ask an adult about opening a bank account. If you want to withdraw money regularly, choose a checking account, also known as a current or transaction account. It will keep your money safer than a piggy bank, but still give you regular access to it.

LONG-TERM SAVING

If you want to save for the more distant future, find out about bank savings accounts. These let you make fewer withdrawals but pay you higher interest, which helps your savings grow—or, at least, not lose value due to inflation.

For the really long term—such as saving for college—financial institutions may offer low-tax or tax-free saving schemes. Some invest your money in shares (see page 122). These accounts take less tax from the interest you earn, but they may not let you withdraw anything until you're an adult.

OUT OF CURIOSITY

Adults in European countries such as Luxembourg, Switzerland, and Sweden are among the biggest savers. On average, they save more of their income than people in other countries.

MAKE A STATEMENT

With most accounts, banks send regular statements, which are messages listing deposits and withdrawals. If you are saving in a piggy bank, make your own statements by noting down deposits, withdrawals, and your changing balance. Statements help you track your savings as they grow—and watch out for suspicious withdrawals, so you can tell an adult or the bank immediately.

WHY SAVE?

Many adults save so they have a safety net when an unexpected event occurs, such as an illness or a car breaking down. Many also save so they can get together the money for big expenses, such as a trip, the deposit on a new home, or retirement.

As a child, you can save for the same reasons—preparing for the unexpected and working toward your goals. In addition, by learning how to save money now, you are gaining the skills—from monitoring your balance to controlling your spending—that will help you manage your finances when you're an adult.

CREATING A BUDGET

The first step toward saving is to create a budget. A budget is a plan that shows incoming money, outgoing money, and how much money remains to be spent or saved. Even if you're not saving, managing your budget is a key skill.

BUDGETING TO SAVE

To create a budget, try using a notebook where you can track your income (money coming in) and **expenditure** (money spent) over a certain period of time, such as a month.

1. Gather your paperwork, including receipts and bank statements or your own "piggy bank statements."

2. Add up your income for your chosen period.

3. Add up your expenditure for the same period.

4. Subtract your expenditure from your income. If this leaves you with any money left over, that is the amount you could save.

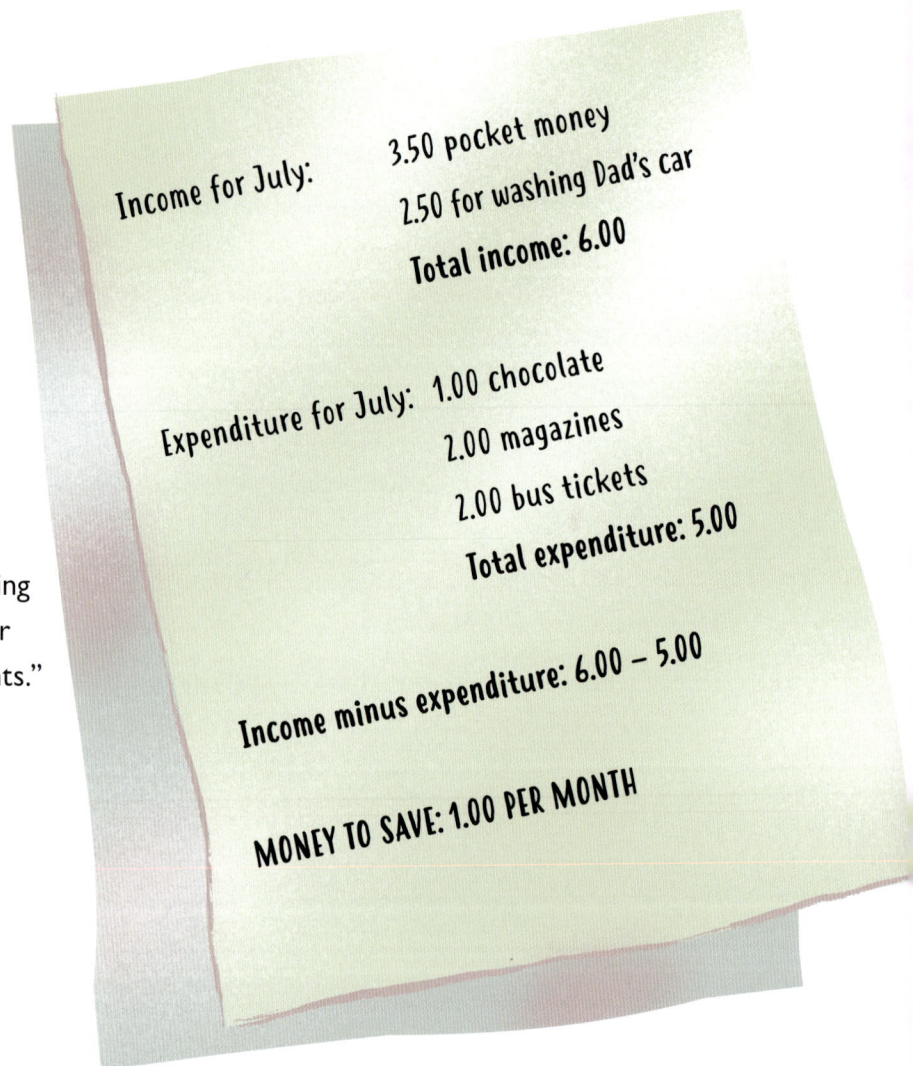

Income for July:
3.50 pocket money
2.50 for washing Dad's car
Total income: 6.00

Expenditure for July:
1.00 chocolate
2.00 magazines
2.00 bus tickets
Total expenditure: 5.00

Income minus expenditure: 6.00 – 5.00

MONEY TO SAVE: 1.00 PER MONTH

OUT OF CURIOSITY

Most governments produce yearly budgets, showing their income and expenditure for the next year, which must be voted on by lawmakers in Congress or Parliament.

WANT TO SAVE MORE?

If your budget does not allow you to save 20 percent of your income, you could increase your income or reduce your expenditure. To increase your income, you could offer to do chores or cooking in exchange for pocket money. To lower your expenditure, look at your receipts to see where you could cut back. For example, if you buy a lot of snacks when you're on the go, try taking food you cooked at home.

SAVINGS

HOW MUCH TO SAVE?

Financial experts encourage adults to save at least 20 percent—a fifth—of their earnings. Many adults are unable to save so much, because paying for essentials takes more than 80 percent of their income. However, we can all keep 20 percent in mind as a goal.

STICK TO YOUR LIMITS

Once you have decided how much you can save, set yourself a weekly or monthly limit for your expenditure. To help you stick to this limit, make a list when you go shopping, then buy only the things that are on the list. Never shop when you're hungry or sad, as these feelings will encourage you to buy to fill your stomach—or your heart!

SETTING GOALS

Saving is a great habit to get into now—because habits are hard to break! But saving can be difficult if you don't have a goal. Try setting yourself a savings goal, such as buying concert tickets or making a donation to charity. Whatever goal you decide on, make sure it is realistic.

MAKE IT REAL

Once you have taken a look at your budget, you can figure out a realistic savings goal. Research the costs of things you could aim for, such as a book, a secondhand scooter, or a charity donation that will pay for a bag of seeds for a farmer.

Now divide the cost of your goal by the amount of money you can save each month. How long will it take to reach the goal? If you can reach it in a year or less while still spending on necessities, it is probably a realistic goal. Now set yourself a date to reach your goal.

BREAK IT DOWN

Break your final goal into mini-goals to make it more approachable. Break the total amount of money into smaller portions, then set these as mini-goals to reach by the end of each week or month. When you meet each mini-goal, give yourself a free or low-cost reward, such as watching an episode of a show you really enjoy.

STAY FOCUSED

Keep yourself motivated to continue saving by focusing on your goal. You could pin up a photo of the scooter or seeds that you want to buy—or of the rock star you want to see perform.

OUT OF CURIOSITY

The most common saving goals for Canadian adults are: retirement, home-buying, home-improvement, education, travel, a new vehicle—and a fund for emergencies.

RECALCULATE YOUR GOALS

If you miss a mini-goal because of overspending or meeting an unexpected cost, don't waste time feeling bad about it. Just recalculate your final goal and mini-goals, either by moving them backward or by saving a little more each week. If you keep on trying, you'll meet your target in the end!

PENSIONS

Most people stop working when they reach a certain age, so they can enjoy a well-earned retirement. But how can a retired person support themselves? Throughout their working life, many people pay into a pension so they can do just that.

WHAT IS A PENSION?

A pension, also known as a retirement or superannuation plan, is a savings plan that a person pays into regularly during their working life. Once they retire, they are usually paid regular amounts for as long as they live. Some plans allow a member of the retired person's family to receive the payments after they die.

GOVERNMENT PENSIONS

In many countries, governments offer a basic pension. Working people usually pay an extra tax, often called social or national insurance, during their working life. When they retire, they receive either a single large payment or, more commonly, regular payments throughout their retirement, usually the same amount for every retiree in the country.

PRIVATE PENSIONS

Since payments from government pensions usually cover only basic needs, many people also have a private pension plan. These are offered by financial institutions such as insurance companies. Plans are also often set up by employers, who make payments into their employees' plans as an added benefit of working for them.

GROWING PENSIONS

The money paid into a pension fund by working people is not left in a bank account—it is invested by fund-managers. This helps the money grow significantly, as long as it is safely and widely invested. The fund may be invested in a range of shares (see page 122), government bonds (see page 49), and buildings (see page 121).

GETTING PAYMENTS

For most private pensions, the size of the payments to a retired person depends on how much they paid in and how much the fund has grown. When a person retires, their pension provider figures out how much they can pay each month based on how long the average person lives—so people who live longer often get more benefit from their pension!

OUT OF CURIOSITY

The first known pensions were paid from 13 BCE to retired Roman soldiers, funded by taxation of Roman citizens.

INSURANCE

Insurance is an agreement between a person and an insurance company: The company promises to pay money if the person experiences particular accidents, emergencies, or losses. Like having savings, having insurance helps people to prepare for the future.

WHAT IS INSURANCE?

An agreement between a customer and an insurance company is called a policy. It states what losses are included in the agreement. The customer is called the policyholder. The policyholder pays the insurance company a regular fee, known as a premium. In return, the company agrees to pay for replacing or fixing property or to give an amount of money in particular circumstances.

TYPES OF INSURANCE

Almost any risk can be insured against—from an earthquake damaging a restaurant to a singer losing their voice—but here are some of the most common types of insurance:

- Home: The policy covers a house and its contents against disasters, damage, and theft.
- Vehicle: This pays for damage to your own vehicle and for damage you cause to another person's vehicle.
- Health: This covers routine and emergency healthcare costs.
- Travel: A policy covers trip cancellations, emergency healthcare, and damaged baggage.
- Life: The insurer will pay an agreed amount to a person's family if they die.

?

OUT OF CURIOSITY
After the United States was hit by Hurricane Katrina in 2005, insurers paid out more than US $40 billion.

IS INSURANCE WORTH IT?

If no loss or emergency ever happens, a policyholder never gets anything in return for their premiums—except peace of mind. However, if a policyholder makes a claim, they may be given more than a lifetime's worth of premiums!

AN INSURANCE POLICY IS LIKE CARRYING AN UMBRELLA EVEN WHEN THE SUN IS OUT: YOU KNOW THAT, IF IT RAINS, YOU WILL BE PROTECTED!

HOW DO INSURERS MAKE MONEY?

Insurers need to make a profit after they have paid out to policyholders. To help with this, they invest the money they take in premiums. They also figure out how much policyholders must pay, by assessing the risk of different events happening. Policyholders who are at higher risk usually pay more, which is why young people—who tend to drive more carelessly—pay more for their car insurance.

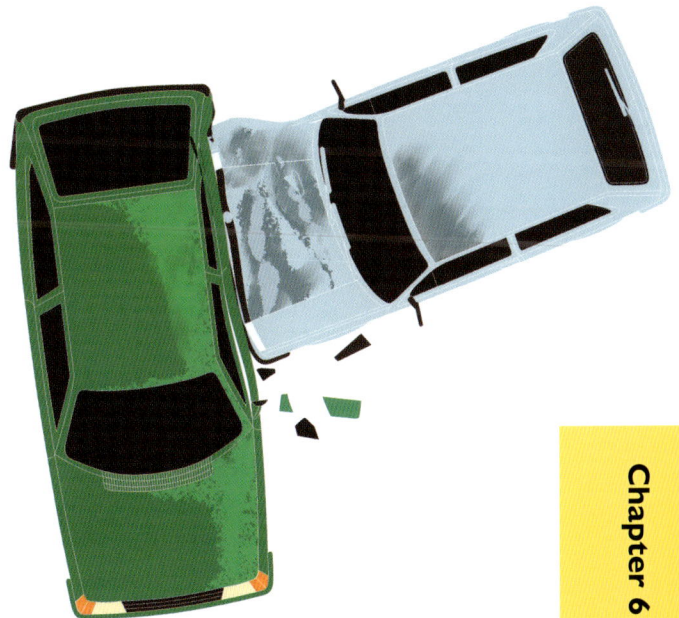

INHERITANCE

When a person dies, the most important thing they leave behind is love! If someone who dies has savings or property, they can leave it—as an inheritance—to family or friends. This is a way for someone to continue caring for the people who are left behind.

WILLS

A will is a legal document that sets out how a person wants their money and property—often called their estate—to be shared after their death. A will is often made with the help of a lawyer.

As well as naming loved-ones in their will, many people leave a gift for a charity. In most countries, a will also names a person, called an executor, who will manage the estate—for example, by selling a house—until it can be distributed.

OUT OF CURIOSITY
The law sees pets as property, so pet-owners can use their will to provide for them, by leaving them to a pet-loving friend or relative.

NO WILLS

Many people do not make a will. This is usually because they are happy for their estate to be shared according to the laws of their country. In most countries, this means that the estate goes to the person's spouse (husband, wife, or—in some countries—their long-term partner) or children. If there is no close family, it passes to more distant relatives.

WHAT'S IN AN INHERITANCE?

An inheritance can include money, property, investments, intangible assets (including patents and trademarks), businesses, and even debts. In most countries, if a person leaves behind only debts, their family cannot be forced to pay them off. However, if a person leaves behind money and property as well as debts, the debts must usually be paid before any money is distributed.

INVESTMENTS

An investment is a commitment of money—usually by buying something—in the hope of gaining more money later. Investments range from apartments to postage stamps. All investments come with a risk, since they can grow in value—or shrink!

TAKING RISKS

Low-risk investments—such as government bonds—tend to give lower returns, which is the amount of profit they are likely to give. High-risk investments—such as currencies—may give higher returns, but may also plummet. Investors are advised to put their money in different types of investments, as well as in bank accounts, so they spread their risk.

FINANCIAL INVESTMENTS

These are some of the most common financial investments:

- Shares: Buying a share means buying a small portion of a business (see page 122).

- Currencies: Currencies, including cryptocurrencies, can be bought when their price is lower, then sold when their value rises.

- Commodities: Investors trade in commodities such as gold, oil, or coffee, which change in value due to supply and demand. However, most investors do not buy the actual commodity, instead buying and selling financial products known as derivatives that change value as the commodities change price (see page 125).

- Bonds: Buying a bond means lending money to a government (see page 49) or business, which pays interest on the loan and repays all the money after a certain time.

- Funds and trusts: These shared "packages" of investments are managed by experts. The experts invest in a range of shares, bonds, commodities, or even buildings. Investors can buy and sell portions of each investment package.

LAND AND BUILDINGS

Some people invest by buying land or buildings, from homes to warehouses. Property, also known as real estate, usually rises in value over a few years or decades, so it may be possible to sell it in the future for more money. Most investors also rent their property to people or businesses to gain a steady income.

COLLECTIBLES

Collectibles are items that people like to collect, including postage stamps, comic books, coins, trading cards, toys, art, and antiques. Investors buy collectibles in the hopes they will rise in value, so they can be sold for a profit. Investors must choose well, as what seems beautiful or fun today may go out of fashion tomorrow.

OUT OF CURIOSITY

In 2017, a painting by Italian artist Leonardo da Vinci (1452–1519) sold for around US $450 million.

STOCKS AND SHARES

Owning a share means that you own a fraction of a particular business. Together, all the shares held by investors make up a business's stock. Investors buy shares in the hopes of making a profit!

OWNING A SHARE

Businesses sell shares to get money for growth. The number of shares in a business is declared at the point the business is formed—or when the business starts to sell shares through a **stock exchange**. If a company is worth $100 million and it sells 100 million shares, each share is worth $1. If you own one share, you own 0.000001 percent of the company.

GETTING DIVIDENDS

Shareholders are regularly paid a fraction of the business's profits, in proportion to the number of shares they own. These payments are called dividends.

PUBLIC AND PRIVATE

There are two main types of shares: private and public. Private businesses usually sell their shares to investors that they know. Public businesses have their shares listed on a stock exchange, which is a share marketplace, so anyone can buy them or sell them to other investors.

Most businesses start out as private, but can apply to a stock exchange to become a listed public company. To protect investors, a business will be accepted only if it is large and well managed. Some companies are listed on one exchange, but multinational companies may be listed on several.

? OUT OF CURIOSITY

One of the world's largest public companies, Apple Inc. was founded in 1976 in the United States and went public in 1980.

SHARE PRICE

When a public company first sells shares, the price of each share is based on the value of the business. After that, as investors buy and sell shares to each other on stock exchanges, the price of each share is whatever an investor will pay on that day.

When lots of people want to buy shares in a successful company, the price goes up, but when lots of investors sell, the price falls. Sometimes, lots of people sell because of worrying world events, from wars to hurricanes.

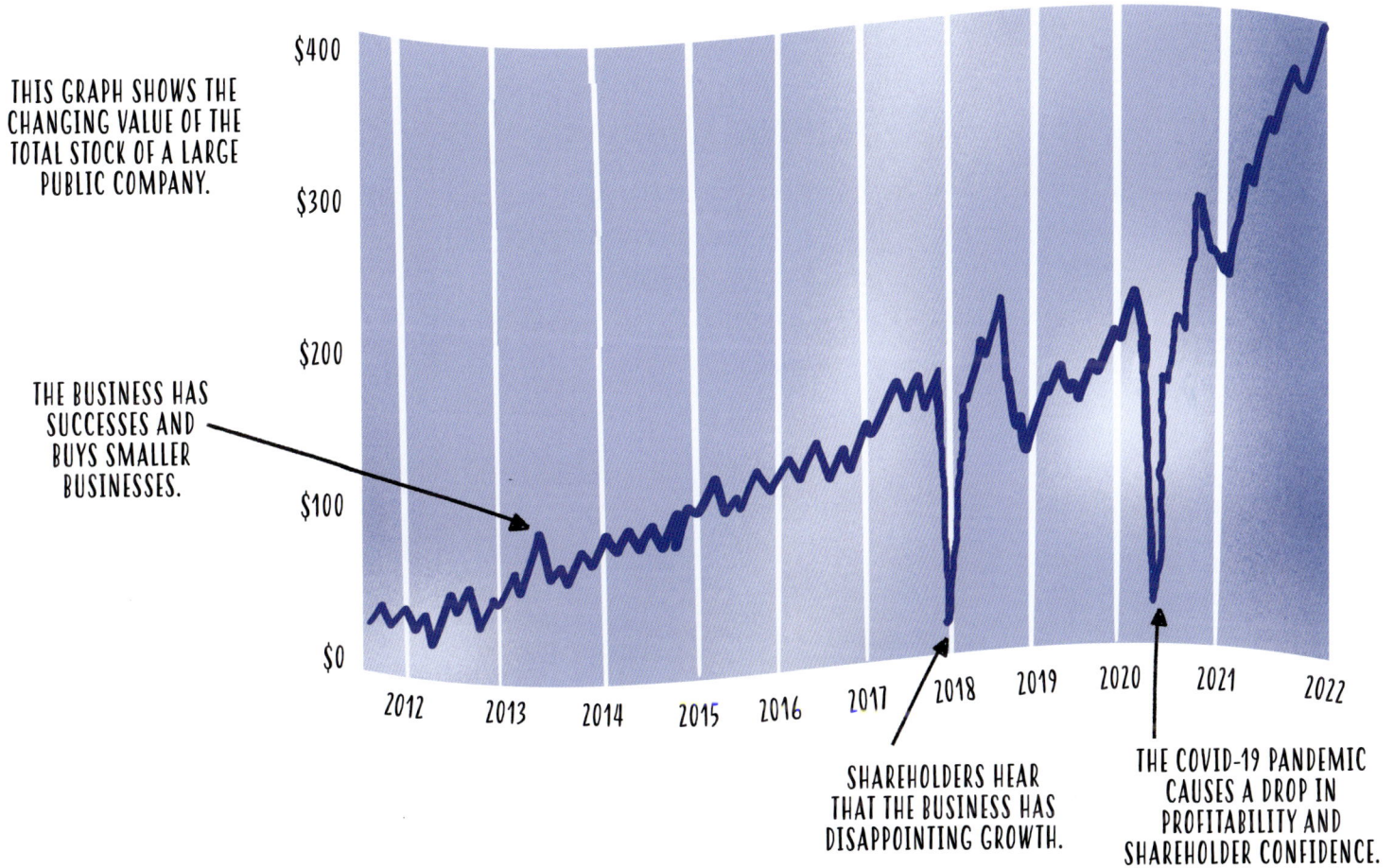

THIS GRAPH SHOWS THE CHANGING VALUE OF THE TOTAL STOCK OF A LARGE PUBLIC COMPANY.

THE BUSINESS HAS SUCCESSES AND BUYS SMALLER BUSINESSES.

SHAREHOLDERS HEAR THAT THE BUSINESS HAS DISAPPOINTING GROWTH.

THE COVID-19 PANDEMIC CAUSES A DROP IN PROFITABILITY AND SHAREHOLDER CONFIDENCE.

HOW DO INVESTORS MAKE A PROFIT?

Investors can make a profit by receiving dividends—and by buying shares when their price is lower, then selling when they rise. However, investors need to know when to sell and when to wait until a slump is over, because mistakes are expensive!

FINANCIAL MARKETS

A financial market is where financial investments, such as shares, are bought and sold. These markets are computerized, so no cash passes from hand to hand! Some, such as the Bombay Stock Exchange, are based in a particular place, while others function only online.

MARKET TRADERS

Only trained and registered traders can buy and sell in most financial markets. Ordinary investors pay a trader, who may be called a broker, to arrange buying and selling for them.

OUT OF CURIOSITY

The largest stock exchange, where the most deals are done, is the New York Stock Exchange, in the United States.

STOCK EXCHANGES

Stock exchanges are where a range of financial investments are traded, including bonds, trusts, and shares of stock in companies listed on that exchange. At some exchanges, traders gather on the trading floor and communicate with words and hand signals. However, many exchanges have switched to a computer-only system.

Share trading follows this process: A buyer bids to buy particular shares at a stated price, while a seller asks to sell those shares at a stated price. When a bid and an ask match, a transaction takes place!

MORE MARKETS

Some financial markets specialize in particular products, including bond, commodity, cryptocurrency, foreign exchange (for currency-trading), and derivatives markets. Derivatives markets, such as the Shanghai Futures Exchange, trade in financial products that are connected to the value of commodities, stocks, bonds, currencies, or interest rates.

Derivatives include futures contracts, which are agreements to buy or sell a particular asset at a set price at a set time. Futures are often bought and sold to hedge (protect against loss). A futures contract might protect an investor in gold from the risk of the price of gold falling, by having an agreement with another investor that they will buy their gold at a high price in six months.

app: A computer program, used on a phone, that can perform particular tasks.

asset: Anything of value that is owned.

automated teller machine (ATM): Also called a cash machine, a machine that is used to withdraw cash when a bank card is inserted.

balance: The amount of money in a bank account.

bank: A business that lends money and keeps safe the money that is paid in by customers.

bank account: An arrangement between a bank and a customer, who can deposit (pay in) and withdraw (take out) their money.

barter: To swap goods or services.

bond: A loan, usually made to a government.

budget: A spending plan.

capital: The money, goods, and materials owned by a business, minus any money owed.

cash: Coins and banknotes.

checking account: Also called a current or transaction account, a type of bank account that allows a customer to make withdrawals whenever they want.

circulation: Money in circulation is being used for buying and selling.

commodity: A material or natural resource, such as wood or gold.

Communist: Governed by the idea that everyone should share their country's land, factories, farms, and wealth.

consumer: A person who buys goods or services for their own use.

counterfeit: Made to be mistaken for something of high value.

credit card: A plastic payment card that allows the holder to borrow money to make purchases, then repay the money later.

cryptocurrency: A currency that exists only on computer systems, relying on secret codes to keep safe records of buying and selling.

currency: A system of money, often using specific banknotes and coins, that is used in a particular country or group of countries.

debit card: A plastic payment card that allows the holder to make purchases.

debt: Money that is owed.

deposit: Money paid into a bank; money paid as the first portion of a larger payment.

digital currency: A currency that is stored and exchanged only on computer systems.

donation: A gift to a charity.

economist: An expert who studies how people, businesses, and countries make money.

economy: How a country's people are making, buying, and sharing goods and services.

electronic money: A record of money that is held on computer systems.

exchange rate: The value at which one currency can be swapped for another.

expenditure: Money spent.

face value: The value printed or stamped on a coin or banknote.

fee: A payment for work or other services.

fiat money: A form of money that has little value in itself but can be used for payments because it is issued by a government.

financial: Relating to money.

financial asset: An asset that is not physical (such as cash or cars), including money in a bank account, bonds, and shares.

fossil fuels: Coal, oil, and natural gas, which release air-heating gases when burned.

goods: Items that are for sale.

hacker: A person who uses computers to get other people's private information.

holographic: Creating images that look three-dimensional rather than flat.

income: Money coming in.

industry: A group of businesses that source similar materials, make similar products, or offer similar services.

inequality: When money or opportunities are not shared equally.

inflation: When the prices of goods and services are rising.

insurance: An agreement that a person, in exchange for paying a fee, will be paid money if they suffer a particular loss.

interest: Money paid regularly at a particular rate for the use of money that has been lent.

investment: Something that is bought in the hopes that it will make money over time.

investor: Someone who puts money into something in order to make a profit.

loan: An amount of money that is borrowed.

medium of exchange: Any item that is accepted as payment for goods and services.

microchip: A small electronic device that can store information.

mint: A place where coins are made.

money supply: All the money that is passing from hand to hand or bank to bank in a country.

mortgage: A loan for buying buildings or land.

patent: The legal right to be the only business that can profit from an invention.

payment terminal: Also called a card machine, this equipment reads the information on a payment card so a cost can be charged to it.

pension: A savings plan that a person pays into regularly during their working life, in return for receiving money after they retire.

percentage: A rate or amount, usually given as a number out of 100.

personal identification number (PIN): A secret number typed in when paying with a card or using an ATM.

product: An item or service that is for sale.

profit: The money gained by a business after paying the costs of making and selling their goods or services.

psychologist: Someone who studies the human mind and emotions.

purchase: To buy something.

radio wave: An invisible form of energy that can carry information through the air.

raw material: A basic material, such as wood, that can be used to make products.

recession: When a country experiences a fall in economic activity, with fewer jobs and fewer goods and services being produced.

rent: A payment to someone for the use of their property, such as a house.

retail bank: A bank that offers services to people and small businesses.

retailer: A person or business that sells goods to people, not to other businesses.

salary: A regular payment made to an employee for their work.

sanitation: Systems for supplying drinking water and taking away waste.

savings: Money kept aside rather than spent.

services: Advice, care, entertainment, or other activities that people need.

share: A portion of a business that can be bought and sold.

slogan: A short, catchy phrase.

stock: All the shares in a business that are owned by investors.

stock exchange: A building or computer system where financial investments—such as shares and bonds—can be bought and sold.

sustainable: Causing little damage to the environment and able to continue for a long time.

tax: The money that governments take from people and businesses to pay for their spending.

technology: The use of scientific knowledge to make products or solve problems.

terms: The conditions of an agreement, such as price and period of time.

territory: An area that is ruled by a country, often one that is far away.

trader: A person who buys and sells.

transfer: To move something, such as money, from one place to another.

United Nations: An international organization that works for peace, safety, and health.

unsecured: When a person borrows money without offering property that will be taken by the lender if the person cannot repay.

withdrawal: Money taken out of a bank account.

INDEX